Michael Jordan: The Inspiring Story of One of Basketball's Greatest Players

An Unauthorized Biography

By: Clayton Geoffreys

Table of Contents

Foreword

When a person is first introduced to the game of basketball, few names of prominent players are mentioned as quickly as that of Michael Jordan. Michael Jordan is often considered one of, if not the greatest to ever play the game of basketball. Even today, people still want to "be like Mike".

While LeBron James' entry into the league in the 21st century has made the title of Greatest of All Time become contested, few can dispute the impact that Jordan had on the game. Jordan's dynamic play throughout his career invigorated the Chicago Bulls dynasty as Jordan led the franchise to six different Championship titles.

In this newly revised edition, we explore Michael's story even further to learn about his innate competitive drive and how he exemplified greatness every time he stepped onto the basketball court. Thank you for purchasing *Michael Jordan: The Inspiring Story of One of Basketball's Greatest Players*. In this unauthorized biography, we will learn Michael Jordan's incredible life story and impact on the game of basketball. Hope you enjoy and if you do, please do not forget to leave a review!

Also, check out my website to join my exclusive list where I let you know about my latest books. To thank you for your purchase, I'll gift you free copies of some of my other books at **claytongeoffreys.com/goodies**.

Or, if you don't like typing, scan the QR code here to go there directly.

Cheers,

Clayton Geoffreys

Visit me at www.claytongeoffreys.com

Introduction

There are a few people whose names are synonymous with the sport they play. When we think about boxing, we think of Muhammad Ali. When we talk about baseball, we remember Babe Ruth. And when it comes to the game of basketball, there is only one name we can think of that best defines what the sport is all about—Michael Jordan.

Michael Jordan has always been an icon in basketball. He is widely regarded as the greatest of all time or at least one of the greatest players who have ever played the sport of basketball. That is why we often associate Michael Jordan with basketball even though it has been more than two decades since he left the Chicago Bulls in 1998 to retire for the second time in his career.

There's a reason why Jordan built up one of the greatest careers that anyone has ever seen, not only in the NBA but throughout professional sports. MJ changed the way the game was played and captivated different fans and fellow players alike with his different brand of basketball and the spunk and sheer confidence he exuded whenever he was on the court.

Before Jordan, shooting guards and swingmen were never really regarded as truly dominant players who could take over games in an instant. Shooting guards were merely asked to shoot, as the name of the position implies. While there were some really good shooting guards such as Sam Jones, Gail Goodrich, and "Pistol" Pete Maravich, they were too far in between and none of them truly had the

3

combination of size, skill, and athleticism that allowed them to take over their own teams as the cornerstones of their franchise.

Taking his cue from the league's first highflying wing, Julius "Dr. J" Erving, Michael Jordan took what his predecessors had and turned it into something better and entirely unique to his own style of play. Jordan made use of his athletic gifts and became a highflying and attacking wing similar to Dr. J himself. However, as he evolved over the years, Jordan became a deadly jump shooter who had the ability to create shots from anywhere on the floor. This allowed him to win an unprecedented and unmatchable total of 10 scoring championships throughout a 15-year career.

Michael Jordan may have been known for his on-the-court exploits as an unstoppable scorer and all-around player but his image was not merely restricted to basketball. His name also transcended into clothing, pop culture, movies, music, and other sports like baseball. However, it all started with everything he's accomplished in basketball—with more than 32,000 points, 6 Most Valuable Player Awards, and several individual distinctions for both offense and defense. He may have been a cultural icon but Michael Jordan was a basketball player first and foremost.

Jordan once said, "The game of basketball has been everything to me. My place of refuge, place I've always gone where I needed comfort and peace. It's been the site of intense pain and the most intense feelings of joy and satisfaction." True enough, basketball was indeed where he felt like he was himself, but he had to leave it back in 1993 when his father passed away and the pressures of the media and society became too heavy for his shoulders to bear. However, he returned shortly thereafter in 1995 after a two-year absence. Proving that he was still "the man," Jordan dominated the league and led the Chicago Bulls to the NBA's first-ever 70-win team.

In the process of etching his name in the basketball records with his amazing scoring feats and individual accomplishments, Michael Jordan was able to win six NBA championships on two separate three-peats. And, in his final year with the Chicago Bulls before retiring for the second time in his career, he made the most memorable shot of his life by draining a game-winner that sealed his sixth NBA championship.

Michael Jordan returned to the NBA in 2001 as a 38-year old playing against the younger generation of shooting guards. Nevertheless, he still proved himself to be more than capable of handling an NBA grind and to score over any defense as he averaged more than 20 points per game over the next two seasons with the Washington Wizards. He finally retired from the game for good in 2003 and was tied with Wilt Chamberlain for the highest all-time career points per game average.

Leaving the game as a winner both on and off the court and as a household name who inspired an entire generation while changing the culture of the game of basketball, Michael Jordan is still widely

5

regarded as the GOAT—or the *greatest of all time*—not only because of the stats he put up and the awards he racked up but also because of how much of a global icon he was and still is. That is why a lot of kids today still dream of becoming "like Mike."

Chapter 1: Childhood and Early Life

The story of every legend starts from a beginning in humbler times, and for Michael Jeffrey Jordan, his story began when he was born on February 17, 1963, in Brooklyn, New York, as the fourth of five children. A few years after Michael was born, his parents, James and Deloris, were worried about the negative impact of exposing their children to the mean streets of Brooklyn, which brought temptations of drugs, alcohol, and violence to impressionable young minds. Thus, the family made the move to Wilmington, North Carolina, a much smaller, quieter town that they perceived to be better for raising a family.

This would be the home of the Jordan family. His father James worked at an electric plant and his mother Deloris worked at a bank. Michael had two older brothers, Larry and James Jr., an older sister, Deloris, and a younger sister, Roslyn. His parents focused on showing their children an eagerness to work and achieve their goals.

Early in life, Michael played sports for fun. However, he would often feel discouraged because his older brother Larry surpassed him a good majority of the time. His father also felt that Larry, who was one year older than Michael, had the real basketball talent in the family. Still, the two would play and invent their own types of games in their giant backyard that included about 5 acres of land and 13 additional acres owned by family.

Part of the reason Michael's father felt Larry had the talent was because Michael was not very tall in his younger years and there was not any sign of that changing since no one in the family had ever reached six feet in height.

Larry was one of Michael's best influences in basketball. As mentioned, he and Mike often had plenty of battles back on their property. Being the bigger brother back then by virtue of the fact that he was about a year older, Larry often beat Michael. Their battles were both physical and competitive. But Michael, even at such a young age, was driven to win—he did not let Larry stop playing until he won against the older brother. To that end, their mother often had to intervene just so they would stop playing.[i]

Michael also got his inspiration for the number 23 from Larry. When he was playing organized basketball, Larry Jordan wore the number 45, which Mike would later use at one point in his career. Because Michael wanted to be half as good as his brother, he used the number 23 for his jersey. Of course, he rounded it up because he could not wear 22.5.[i]

Larry Jordan turned out to be quite the basketball player in high school but he just was not cut out to play the sport at a high level because of his lack of height. As mentioned, the Jordans were never a tall family. Larry stayed at about 5'8" throughout his entire life and was never tall enough to compete against bigger players in the professional ranks. However, Michael and their father James agreed that Larry would have been just as good and possibly even better than Michael had he been taller.[ii]

Mike's other brother, James Jr., found success in life, but not as an athlete. He joined the U.S. Army and was part of the 35th Signal Brigade that fell under the XVIII Airborne Corps. He had a long military career that lasted until 2006 when he retired as a command sergeant major. According to James Sr., it was Junior, or Ronnie, as the family loved calling him, who possessed the best leadership skills out of all the Jordan siblings.[iii]

Michael Jordan continued to play football, baseball, and basketball during his childhood. Interestingly enough, his favorite sport was not basketball at the time. He enjoyed baseball the most. When he was 12, he was named a top player in his youth league for his play both on the pitching mound and in the outfield. He was also named Most Valuable Player when he represented his team in a state tournament.

Back then, Michael was not a "clean-cut" boy but a mischievous one with a penchant for getting into trouble. In fact, he was suspended at age 12 for fighting and had also been in other bouts in the halls up until that point.[ii] His mother, Deloris, did not let him sit at home and watch TV when he was not at school. She took him with her to work and made him sit in the car all day to read—within perfect view from the bank window. After work, his mother took him to the library where she had a friend who worked there and made sure that he did even more reading.

Michael often complained about the punishment later in life, protesting that he was not allowed to have fun back then. But Deloris knew better. The punishment served as a precedent of what she was capable of as a mother if one of her children caused some trouble again. From then on, Michael Jordan never caused the family any more trouble.[ii]

Speaking of family, togetherness was always one of the most important aspects that kept the Jordan family together. Both James and Deloris always made it a point that each of their children would attend the activities of one another for support. This became a family rule in the Jordan household. And the best part was that no one was jealous of the other because the siblings worked hard to hone their own individual talents.

Deloris always preached to her children that all of them had unique talents of their own. Larry may have been the better basketball player at first, but more than that, he was better than anyone else when it came to knowing what to do with his hands in terms of fixing things. The oldest son Ronnie (James Jr.) was a born leader. Meanwhile, Roslyn was a good storyteller.[iii]

As for Michael, he may not have been the best Jordan at basketball back when he was a young boy, but he always had an inkling that basketball was where he truly belonged, despite his love of baseball. Basketball was what he wanted to be good at and it was something he pursued with all his heart when he got to high school.

As a middle school student at D.C. Virgo Preparatory Academy, 15-year-old Michael was an all-around athlete playing three different sports. However, he was not fanatical about any of them. No one imagined that he would have a career in sports as he entered high school at Emsley A. Laney High School, which was a bumpy road in itself but helped the young heir of NBA royalty get started.

High School Years

The start of Michael Jordan's high school basketball career in 1978 did not go as he expected. He hoped to fill the extra roster spot on the varsity team for the Buccaneers' playoff season during his sophomore year. However, they went with his friend, Harvest Leroy Smith, and the decision made sense. Jordan was only 5'10" and his friend Leroy was nearly six-and-a-half-feet tall, a good trait for high school basketball. Jordan, at the time, was also just a little above average in shooting and was mediocre on defense. He was instead relegated to the junior varsity team by Coach Clifton "Pop" Herring.

Meanwhile, it was his brother Larry who dominated and starred for their high school team even though he may have been a bit shorter than Michael by that time. During those years, Larry was indeed well above Michael in terms of school athletics as he was able to star for the very same team that cut his younger brother out partly due to his lack of height. Larry was only 5'8" while Michael was 5'10". And at the same time, the taller Leroy Smith was able to turn himself into a productive player as well, largely thanks to his height of 6'4".[iii]

While most of us know the legend of Jordan, not a lot of people know that his friend Leroy Smith had some success of his own in the sport. Eventually, the sophomore who beat out the soon-to-be NBA champion would accept a four-year athletic scholarship to play basketball for the University of North Carolina in Charlotte—not the same as the team that wears the iconic "Tar Heel" blue and white. Rather, it was the green and gold of the Charlotte 49ers; Leroy became their senior captain and led all teams in the Sun Belt Conference in rebounding. After that, Smith would spend the mid-1980s and into the early 1990s playing for various clubs in the Premier English Basketball League, the German Basketball League, the United States Basketball League, and the Japanese (Nippon) Basketball League. While he was a team leader in points, rebounds, and blocks, Leroy never made the move to the NBA and he would find himself transitioning into the business world to become the vice president of sales and marketing for NBC Universal's TV Distribution.

When Michael Jordan learned that he did not make the varsity team, he did what any normal teenager would do—he ran back home and locked himself in his room to cry.[iv] Yes, the untouchable man known as Michael Jordan cried his heart out when he thought that he would not be able to achieve his dreams after getting cut from his high school team. And the reason why he was not able to get to that level was because he was only 5'10" and not athletic enough to dunk. He was still far from being the 6'6" legend known for having one of the highest-recorded vertical leaps in the history of the NBA.

Mike told his mother that he wanted to be tall so that he could compete against the bigger boys in his high school and perhaps make the team. Still, given the fact that none of his family members were close to six feet tall, the possibility seemed unlikely. Michael, at age 15, was the tallest in the family at 5'10". His father was about 5'7" while his brothers stood somewhere close to that. Mike's genetics were not in his favor, needless to say.

Deloris, who knew that the odds were against Michael, told her son the silliest thing when she said that he should put salt in his shoes and pray so that he would become taller. She did not exactly believe in what she said but she only told her son to do so in an attempt to pacify him whenever they were having dinner. However, she did actually include this story in one of the children's books she would later write. Meanwhile, James Sr. did not know exactly what to say to his son but he did tell Michael that being tall was within himself and that he would be as tall as he wanted to be if he believed in himself.[iii]

Regardless of how he lacked the height to play for his high school varsity team, it was the loss of that varsity spot that caused things to turn around as Jordan took the bad news and made it his motivation to improve for next year and work harder on his basketball skills. He spent every day practicing with his brother Larry.

Larry was always the better player even though he was shorter than his younger brother. The two battled a lot while Michael was trying to prove himself capable enough as a player even though he did not have the height that allowed him to play on his high school team. Larry said that he often dominated Mike back when they were in high school until his little brother was not so little anymore. Michael Jordan started growing.

Michael Jordan was also lucky enough to have a cousin who was tall enough to help him improve in the sport. The cousin, a tall 6'7" youngster, was proof that tallness was actually somewhere deep in the Jordan bloodline and that Mike could have possibly inherited it as well, even though none of his immediate family members were tall. Indeed, the tall genes were somewhere in him just waiting to come out at the right time.

Michael Jordan grew an additional five inches to become 6'3" between his sophomore and junior years. His work ethic was evident as he was first in line at the conditioning drills and he ran as hard as anyone, which coaches tend to notice, more so, if it's a player that they didn't select—they are happy to see someone use it as motivation rather than taking it negatively.

During that sophomore season, Jordan improved greatly and was one of the reasons people came to the JV games that were played a few hours prior to the varsity match-up. These included a few games where he scored more than 40 points each. The first of those games was on December 5th, where Jordan scored 45 points in the team's win over East Carteret. Nearly two months later, Jordan scored 44 points to help the team defeat Southern Wayne on January 29th.

Fans were coming out to see Jordan score a lot of points as he was becoming a star player even without being part of the evening varsity main event game—whether he was scoring 24 points against East Carteret on December 15th, or only scoring 6 points against New Hanover on February 16th, fans wanted to see Jordan entertain with his emerging skills and hustle on every play.

Despite the impressive numbers Jordan was putting up and the attention he was bringing for the junior varsity squad, he never got a call-up during his sophomore year. It only inspired Jordan to become even more competitive.

However, during his junior year, he got the call. He was ready to play for the varsity team not only because he was considerably taller than he was when he first tried out but also because he was significantly better overall—all in only the span of a single year. At that point, even Larry Jordan went on to say that his younger brother was now better than him. Larry was still a formidable player, however, and it was not until Michael outgrew him by a lot that he was able to dominate his older brother in pickup games. This was the only year that Michael and Larry were teammates.

During his junior season with the varsity team, Jordan would average close to 25 points per game for a 4-A team, which was North Carolina's highest classification. In his first game at the varsity level, Jordan scored 35 points in a win against Pender High School on November 30th. A few games later, Jordan scored 28 points in a loss to Southern Wayne on December 11th. He then scored 31 points against Kinston on December 18th in a win. After that, Jordan scored 29 and 30 points against New Bern and Wadesboro-Bowman respectively.

He next scored 40 points after hitting 17 total field goals in a losing effort on January 2, 1980, against Goldsboro. A few months later, he scored a season high of 42 points on February 14th in a win over Eastern Wayne. This was right before Jordan helped the Laney Buccaneers to the North Carolina Division II Playoffs where he scored 20 points in the team's win over Southern Wayne. At the end of the year, Jordan had played 22 total games and averaged 24.8 points per game as the Buccaneers finished with a varsity record of 14-10. He would continue to improve and was starting to collect a following of several college basketball programs in the region.

In the summer that followed, he dazzled college scouts while attending Howard Garfinkel's Five-Star Basketball Camp, often playing with other top high school players one-on-one. He led his high school to the No. 1 state ranking in his final year with the Buccaneers and finished the season with a record of 19-4 in the 1980-1981 season.

They would win their first five games, including Jordan scoring 33 points in the season opener against Pender on November 26, 1980, followed by a road win over the same Pender team on December 5th where Jordan scored 27 points on 12 field goals. Jordan scored another 21 points in the Buccaneers' December 9th win over Southern Wayne and 28 points in a close victory on the road at Hoggard on December 12th.

As the season continued, Jordan reached the 30-point mark a total of six times, highlighted by his performance on February 3, 1981, where he finished a win over Kinston with 39 points. Just like the previous season, the Buccaneers were led by Jordan to the state's Division II Playoffs that started with a 55-28 dominant win on February 23rd over Eastern Wayne. Jordan scored 27 points in that game just three days after scoring 26 points against the same team in a win to end the regular season. But once again, Jordan and his Laney teammates were unable to win the state championship after a loss to New Hanover in the conference title game.

As a senior in 1981, Jordan was selected to the All-American team after averaging a triple-double, with 29.2 points, 11.6 rebounds and 10.1 assists per game. Jordan also joined his school's 1,000-point club with 1,165 points in his senior season. But Jordan was not done with high school basketball as he was part of a couple of national All-Star games. It started on March 26th during the McDonald's Capital Classic in Landover, Maryland where Jordan was part of the United team that defeated Capital. He finished with 14 points in a game that also featured Jordan being on the opposite side of names like Patrick Ewing and Lorenzo Gill.

A few days later, Jordan would receive a chance to play in the annual All-American Game in Wichita, Kansas. It was a consolation game of sorts for the young Jordan, who scored 30 points and received the game's Most Valuable Player Award after making the final two free throws with 11 seconds left to clinch the win for the East over the West.

In the summer months before going to play college basketball, Jordan was also part of a South All-Star team that competed in the National Sports Festival in Syracuse, New York that ran July 25-29th. Jordan's team finished 2-2 in the four games, including an 18-point performance in the South's win over the East on July 26th.

Michael Jordan also played baseball in high school where he pitched 45 consecutive innings without allowing a run. His talents attracted offers not only from college basketball programs, but also from baseball programs at various Division I schools, including Duke University, the University of South Carolina, Syracuse University, and the University of Virginia. However, one of the most prominent names in the recruitment pitch was North Carolina's Dean Smith.

The recruitment actually started when Jordan was still a junior in high school. North Carolina assistant Roy Williams received a call from the athletic director over at Hanover County, who told him that there was an interesting young man named Michael Jordan, a 6'4" athletic junior who could possibly become a star not only in college but in the NBA as well. North Carolina's head basketball coach, Dean Smith, sent a scouting coach over to watch Jordan's games. However, the coach came back and told Smith and Williams that, while Michael Jordan was indeed athletic, he seemed much more interested in taking long jumpers than using his physical tools near the basket. To that end, Smith and the rest of the North Carolina coaching staff were not particularly enthused by what Jordan had to offer.[v]

But that was not the end of it. When Michael Jordan attended a summer camp a year before his senior season, Roy Williams was still intrigued enough that he managed to be there to see for himself what the lanky 6'4" junior was all about. It was then and there when he was impressed by what Jordan could do. He repeatedly asked Michael Jordan to play longer than he needed to because Williams wanted to make sure that this young man was good enough to play for North Carolina in Chapel Hill. Sure enough, he loved what Jordan brought to the table—little did he know, this kid was going to be the greatest of all time! Thankfully, Dean Smith and North Carolina made the recruitment pitch that ultimately brought Michael Jordan over to Chapel Hill the next year.[v]

On a side note, Jordan accepted the UNC scholarship and chose cultural geography as his college major, which is where one studies things in culture and how they adjust to their specific locations and other factors like religion, language, government, and economy. While this was likely not just an easy major to coast through classes for eligibility, there was a good chance that Jordan was hoping basketball would work out for him and his studies were more a hobby-like interest.

Chapter 2: College Years at UNC

Freshman Year

Being in North Carolina was a good thing for Michael Jordan because he had a chance to join Dean Smith and learn from him. In college basketball circles, Smith was widely regarded as one of the very best. He began his head coaching career in North Carolina back in 1961. And, prior to Jordan's arrival to Chapel Hill, he coached his Tar Heels team to 11 NCAA Tournament appearances while making it to the Final Four six times. However, his tenure in North Carolina had yet to produce a national title that would solidify his name as one of the greatest college coaches of all time.

When Jordan joined the team, the Tar Heels already had two terrific players who would become solid NBA players. Future Hall-of-Famer James Worthy, who would later win multiple titles with the Los Angeles Lakers in the NBA, was a junior who had averaged 14 points in the previous season. Meanwhile, another future Laker, Sam Perkins, was also capable of putting up 14 points a night in Dean Smith's balanced offensive attack. Both Worthy and Perkins were the alphas of that team. In that sense, Jordan was coming in as a freshman who would have to find his place behind two players who had already established themselves in the system.

In a press conference before the season started, Dean Smith introduced his players in a way that fits his status as one of the best coaches in the collegiate ranks. He explained to the media the areas that his players had worked on and how they improved. On speaking about the incoming rookie named Michael Jordan, Smith was high on his quickness and espoused how he believed that this young freshman was going to be a good defensive player and a capable shooter by working hard on his game. But the one point that stood out the most was that Dean Smith said Jordan himself recognized that he still had a lot to learn at that point in his career.[vi]

Nevertheless, Michael Jordan had a very good year as a young star out of Wilmington, North Carolina, which is about 162 miles north of the University of North Carolina campus in Chapel Hill. It was another 879 miles to where the newest Tar Heel would take his first step in establishing himself as a clutch-shooter in key moments—at his college debut in the Tar Heels' win over the University of Kansas Jayhawks during the season opener on November 28, 1981.

While Jordan missed his first shot as a college basketball player, he would make the next 3 as he scored 12 points while making 5 out of 10 shots from the field. It would only take only a few games before Jordan surpassed the 20-point mark as a Tar Heel, with 22 points after making 11 out of 15 field goals in the team's win over Tulsa in what would be his high in scoring for the season.

In Jordan's first year at Chapel Hill, the Tar Heels finished the regular season with the No. 1 ranking in both the Coaches and Associated Press polls after a 32-2 record, 12-2 in the Atlantic Coast Conference.

The team would go three for three en route to a conference championship win over third-ranked Virginia on March 7, 1982.

As successful as Michael Jordan already was at such an early point in his freshman year, he was still one of the most hard-working players any coach could find. Assistant coach Roy Williams once said that Jordan told him that he wanted to be the best to ever play the game. To that, Williams told Mike that he not only needed to work as hard as anyone else, but he also needed to work harder than everyone if he wanted to be special. Michael Jordan told the assistant coach that he will never question his work ethic ever again.[vi]

Already athletic and talented, MJ had the same work ethic that he had when he was still a high school sophomore trying to make his prep school's varsity team. The one thing that a coach needed from his superstar was the desire to get better than he already was. This was what allowed the North Carolina Tar Heels to succeed even when Jordan was still a freshman.

The Tar Heels continued their success during the 1982 NCAA National Championship Tournament and started with a second-round game against James Madison where Jordan made about three out of eight field goals (37.5%) for a finish of six rebounds and one rebound in the team's 52-50 win. By that time, no one could question that the North Carolina Tar Heels that season was a special squad led by incredibly talented players who had what it took to give the team a title.

In the Sweet 16 round of the tournament, they notched an impressive, hard-fought win over Alabama. The starting five were able to step up with little support—only two points coming off of the bench. All of North Carolina's starters scored double figures, with Worthy and Matt Doherty each scoring 16 points, followed by Perkins' 15, and Jimmy Black contributing 14 points.

Jordan would also score double digits in North Carolina's Elite Eight matchup with the Villanova Wildcats, who were a third-seed with 22 wins. Jordan finished with 15 points to be the Tar Heels' leading scorer in a win that took the North Carolina Tar Heels all the way to the Final Four yet again under the tutelage of Dean Smith.

In the Final Four game against Houston, Jordan continued to perform well, finishing with 18 points. The Tar Heels took the win and were headed to the NCAA Finals in just Mike's first season with North Carolina. Coincidentally, that Houston team featured future NBA legends Clyde Drexler and Hakeem Olajuwon, a pair that Jordan would also have plenty of NBA battles with in the future. But, at that moment, Michael Jordan had a date with Patrick Ewing's Georgetown Hoyas in the NCAA Finals.

North Carolina trailed Georgetown 62-61 with 32 seconds left in front of 61,612 fans during the NCAA Championship game at the Louisiana Superdome in New Orleans. Both sides featured players who would have great careers in the National Basketball Association a few years later. The Hoyas featured Patrick Ewing, another

24

freshman who scored 23 points. Meanwhile, the Tar Heels had the junior James Worthy, who was well on his way out of college, Sam Perkins, and the freshman sensation named Michael Jordan.

Heading into those last 32 seconds, no team had led by more than a few points down the stretch, and the Tar Heels were able to grab the ball from an inbound pass. Head coach Dean Smith had never won a national championship in the 21 years since he took charge of the program (after spending a combined eight years as an assistant at Kansas, Air Force, and North Carolina). He drew up a play that would put the ball in Jordan's hands, trusting him to take the shot if he found himself open.

Teammate Jimmy Black attracted the defense on the right wing, found Jordan on the left wing, who hit the go-ahead jumper for the 63-62 lead with 17 seconds left—possibly the most important field goal that Jordan made amongst the 7 out of 13 field goals he made that night. Georgetown then turned the ball over, which led to a foul on Worthy, who missed both free throws. Fortunately, the Hoyas had no timeouts and missed a final desperation heave. Smith's decision to give the ball to the youngest Jordan, rather than to Worthy or Perkins, worked for the best and it became the turning point in Jordan's basketball career. It was not going to be Michael Jordan's only game-winning shot in what would become a legendary basketball career.

Jordan had a good season in his first year at UNC—13.5 points per game over 34 games and shooting 53.4% from the field. He finished the 1981-1982 season as the ACC Freshman of the Year but his biggest moment of the year came during that national championship game. He had already accomplished a goal that not many college basketball stars have even gotten close to achieving. That NCAA title paved the way for what was destined to be a season full of championships for the young Michael Jordan.

Sophomore Year

After winning the national championship, the Tar Heels bid goodbye to James Worthy, who was headed to the NBA and would go on to have a legendary career with the Los Angeles Lakers. By parting ways with one of the program's best players, Dean Smith was now able to focus more on the growing and improving Michael Jordan, who had reached his mature height of 6'6" by that time. The lanky wing still needed to work on a lot of areas in his game even if he did indeed hit that game-winning shot to give the team the national title.

Before the season began, and just after the Tar Heels won the 1982 NCAA Championship, Michael Jordan came into Dean Smith's office for a customary meeting. One of the things that Smith was known for was his ability to treat his players equally, regardless of whether it was the Tar Heels' best scorer or the one sitting at the end of the bench. He was also well-known for keeping an eye on his players' development and making sure that he had a hand at making everyone under him better. This included Michael Jordan.

When Jordan entered Smith's office, he was told that he needed to improve on three key parts of his game: shooting, passing, and defense. Michael, a scorer who drove hard to the basket almost every time, was never really known to be the deadliest shooter. But he was someone who shot the ball from midrange really well and would be especially dangerous from it later on in his career. It was with Dean Smith that he started working on his shooting mechanics. Of course, we all know how terrific a playmaker and defender Jordan later became when he got to the NBA.

In his sophomore season, Jordan finished with an average of 20.0 points per game in 36 games and shot more than 53% from the field. (If you followed Jordan's early career, it may bring to mind an old running joke that Dean Smith himself—who in truth would become Jordan's greatest and most beloved mentor) was the only one who could hold MJ under 20 points.) Jordan also increased his rebounding average from 4.4 per game as a freshman to five and a half per game.

The Tar Heels finished the year 28-8 with a 12-2 record in the ACC. However, they were unable to make a repeat as the ACC Tournament champions after losing to North Carolina State in overtime on March 12th. They finished as the eighth-ranked team in the nation, earning a second-seed in the NCAA Tournament.

It was a rough start to the season after starting third in the polls and falling to 15th after losing to St. John's University and to Missouri. After a 3-3 start, however, they got back on track. UNC went on to win 18 games in a row, and while they lost three games in a row to Villanova, Maryland, and North Carolina State, they finished up the regular season with four straight ACC conference games, including a win over one of their fiercest rivals, Duke.

The Tar Heels then made an appearance in the ACC Conference Tournament in an attempt to earn their conference's automatic bid in the National Championship. Things were looking good after earning a blowout victory over the Clemson Tigers on March 11th, but they were unable to continue that momentum when they lost to their in-state foes, the North Carolina State Wolfpack.

While the Tar Heels were unable to claim the ACC's one automatic berth to the championship tournament, North Carolina would return to the NCAA Tournament as a team that earned an at-large bid, which is given to a team that finishes 26-7 against the tough competition found throughout the entire Atlantic Coast Conference.

One year after winning the national championship as the top seed overall, the North Carolina Tar Heels found themselves as the second seed coming out of the East Region. While it felt like a familiar place being a favorite in the opening game of their tournament, they also found themselves up against a familiar rival, James Madison University, who only lost by two points against North Carolina in their second-round game in the 1982 tournament. The result was the same as in 1983. While the score was different, the Tar Heels took the win with Jordan playing a support role for that game only.

After making it all the way to the Sweet 16 yet again, the Tar Heels followed that up with a win in that round against third-seeded Ohio State. Although Michael Jordan was the leading scorer among the North Carolina blue and whites, he struggled from the field, making only 5 out of 15 shots.

The Tar Heels were looking strong at the right time and experts were starting to wonder, many second-guessing what they previously projected early on in the month. However, the Tar Heels ended up losing to the University of Georgia in the East Regional Finals. The loss was not entirely the fault of Jordan as he went on to finish that game with 26 points.

Georgia fell to the eventual champions from North Carolina State in the next round, the same ACC team that prevented the Tar Heels from advancing in the conference tournament earlier that month. While the team didn't win the national championship, Jordan found that he had a slight improvement in his shooting efficiency. From shooting 53.5% field goals, Jordan reached per game averages of 20 points (a huge jump from the 13.5 points per game in his freshman season) with 5.5 rebounds, 2.2 steals, 1.6 assists, and just under one blocked shot per game. The individual numbers were good enough to help Jordan find a spot in the First Team All-American list.

After their loss in the East Regional Finals and failing to secure a consecutive NCAA championship, Michael Jordan found himself on the receiving end of another lecture from Dean Smith, who believed his star player still had a lot of things he could work on. But, instead of asking MJ to go to his office, Smith wrote him a personal letter that detailed everything that the Tar Heel star needed to work on to become a better player in time for his junior season.

Dean Smith saw the problems in Jordan's game and made sure his pointers would help his star player. He detailed the things that Michael needed to do as follows:

1. Shoot the ball with the same arc consistently every time.
2. Avoid fading back with his body when shooting a free throw.
3. Play point guard during pick-up games to improve his dribbling and passing while learning how to reduce his turnovers in the process.
4. Learn how to utilize ball fakes when making plays for others.
5. Know how to use his athletic ability after a rebound to take the ball coast to coast all by himself.
6. Work on using his pivot foot well.
7. Stay consistent with his defensive habits to develop into an elite defender.
8. Minimize gambling for steals and try to contain his defensive assignment instead.

At the end of the note, Dean Smith told Jordan that if he would be able to work on those parts of his game, he will become a better player and their team will also benefit a lot from his development.[vii] What Smith did not know was that Jordan not only worked on those parts of his game but also used them as the roots of his fundamentals when he got to the NBA.

Jordan, in the NBA, eventually became a consistent shooter both from the floor and from the free-throw line, developed into a great playmaker at the shooting guard spot, turned into a phenomenal athlete at taking the ball all the way to the other end, used his pivot foot at the post better than any guard ever did, and ended his career as one of the greatest perimeter defenders of all time. That is precisely why Michael Jordan said that he would not have been what he was in the NBA had it not been for Dean Smith.

Junior Year

Jordan played just as well in his junior year and joined the NCAA All-American First Team again with 19.6 points per game average and shooting a tad over 55% from the field in a 31-game season. He was named the winner of the Dr. James Naismith Award for being the outstanding male basketball player by the Atlanta Tipoff Club, an award named in honor of the inventor of basketball. Jordan also received the John Wooden Award that same year by the Los Angeles Athletic Club, an award named in honor of a legendary player and coach who earned a total of 11 NCAA championships.

Early on, Jordan scored 28 points off the bat in a non-conference game at home against Chattanooga on November 11, 1983. He would regularly score beyond the 20-point mark in the season with 19 games where he scored at least 20 points. His best individual performance came on February 2, 1984, in a win over North Carolina State where Jordan had 32 points. He was close to that 30-point mark a couple more times, including the team's home game win against Louisiana State on January 29th when he had 29 points.

Jordan made plenty of highlights throughout the season, including a breakaway dunk with two seconds left after Perkins blocked a shot in a win at the University of Maryland on January 12th. He looked at the clock before making the exclamation point against the Terrapins with a windmill dunk that acted as a dagger in the hearts of their ACC rivals.

Michael Jordan also earned the ACC Player of the Year, the Adolph Rupp Trophy, and the US Basketball Writers Association's College Player of the Year. North Carolina once again finished with the top ranking in both polls after an overall 28-3 record and going undefeated in ACC action (14-0). It looked as if the Tar Heels were going to have a shot at the ACC's automatic berth into the NCAA National Championship tournament after defeating the Clemson Tigers on March 8th.

However, North Carolina once again failed to win the ACC Tournament after being upset by long-time rival Duke in the semifinal round. Being the top-ranked team in the AP and Coaches' polls for most of the season would likely guarantee a team a spot in the championship tournament. The Tar Heels received the number one seed in the East Regional.

On March 17th the Tar Heels rebounded from that tough loss to Duke in the opening round of the NCAA National Championship Tournament by defeating Temple. This was a game where Jordan scored 27 to lead the team's all-around scoring efforts. It was a good game to advance to the Sweet 16 Round, but North Carolina would lose in the second round to the fourth-seeded Indiana Hoosiers. Jordan didn't have his best game as he only made 6 out of 14 shots from around the court, scoring only 13 points in the game.

After his junior year in college, Michael Jordan was preparing for what could have been his senior year with the North Carolina Tar Heels. However, his head coach intervened in what is still regarded as one of the most unselfish moves a college coach could ever do. At a time when college basketball players did not follow the one-and-done process and would usually stay three to four years with their programs, Dean Smith advised Michael Jordan to forego his final year with the Tar Heels and to declare himself eligible for the NBA.[vii]

For Dean Smith, Michael Jordan no longer had anything else to accomplish in the collegiate ranks. He had won the national title in his freshman season and later became a Player-of-the-Year awardee. Mike was already a winner and an accomplished individual. Smith realized that his best player, and probably the greatest player to have ever donned the Tar Heel colors, needed to go to the NBA because that was what was best for his career.[vii] To that end, Michael Jordan heeded his coach's advice and went on to apply for the NBA draft.

Michael Jordan finished his North Carolina basketball career with plenty of awards and accomplishments. However, arguably the most important gift he got from being a Tar Heel was that he found himself a coach who was like a second father to him. Dean Smith has always had a special place in Jordan's heart and he has said that, other than his parents, his college coach has had the biggest influence in his life. There would be no Michael Jordan without Dean Smith.[vii]

While Jordan continued his basketball career, it's also worth noting that MJ returned to the UNC campus in Chapel Hill, North Carolina to complete his Bachelor's Degree with a major in geography. He wasn't the typical student in North Carolina as he was making highlight plays in the NBA while at the same time taking a variety of college courses that included Elementary Portuguese, Map Interpretation, and Changing Human Environment. He probably thought that it was a great idea to finish his college education in the event that something happened to cause a major setback or premature end to his professional basketball career. However, as it turned out, that would not be a problem; he would not have to use his degree to find work.

Chapter 3: Michael's NBA Career Part I

Getting Drafted

Michael Jordan entered the 1984 NBA Draft, which would later become one of the most successful drafts in the history of the league. Four players from that draft class would turn out to be Hall of Famers. Meanwhile, seven players from that class eventually developed into All-Stars. As such, the class of 1984 is widely regarded as one of the best in history, together with the class of 1996 and the class of 2003.

In the weeks leading up to the draft, anyone might easily consider Michael Jordan as the headliner. After all, he won an NCAA title in only his freshman year and later developed into a Player of the Year awardee in his junior year. In that regard, he came out of North Carolina as one of the most decorated college athletes of that draft class.

However, at that time, the most dominant NBA players were big men. Every champion team had big men that anchored both offense and defense. The recent champions such as the Los Angeles Lakers, Boston Celtics, and the Philadelphia 76ers all had All-Star centers manning their paint. That was why centers were the most important commodities in the NBA back in the 1980s.

To that effect, it was not a surprise that it was Hakeem Olajuwon out of Houston who was considered the consensus top overall pick of the 1984 NBA Draft. At about seven feet tall and with a muscular frame, Olajuwon may not have been playing basketball for a long time at that point but he was already showing the grace, skill level, mobility, and athleticism that could help turn him into a dominant NBA superstar. In his final year in college, he averaged nearly 17 points per game while shooting nearly 70% from the floor. But it was his defensive capabilities that coaches and scouts were high on. That was why he was going to be chosen with the top overall pick.

The Houston Rockets, who already had 7'4" Ralph Sampson, the reigning Rookie of the Year at that time, were looking to solidify their frontline with two seven-footers who could dominate any other big man combination in the league. They went on to draft Hakeem Olajuwon with the first overall pick. Olajuwon would later forge a Hall-of-Fame career for himself as arguably the most skilled center of all time while also finishing as the career leader in blocks.

As Hakeem Olajuwon took the stage as the top overall pick, the second overall pick of the 1984 NBA Draft turned out to become one of the most controversial ones in the entire history of the NBA. The Portland Trailblazers, who owned the second overall pick that year, were up next and were going to make a decision that paved the way for the fate of the NBA itself in a way that would change it towards a different direction.

The Portland Trailblazers were in need of a center at that time. They wanted a big man whom they could rely on for points inside the paint and who was capable enough to defend the basket. And they already had a young guard named Clyde Drexler, who they took from the draft just a year ago. Their wing positions were already solidified and they did not need another wingman to play alongside Jim Paxson and Clyde Drexler.

This is when Sam Bowie entered the picture. At 7'1" and a slender yet mobile frame, Bowie was a talented center back when he was playing for Kentucky. He could run the floor well, move better than most centers, and had the potential to become a star center in the NBA. But there was a red flag—Bowie was injury-prone throughout the five years he spent at Kentucky. He had to sit out two full seasons because of a stress fracture. So, as talented as Sam Bowie was, he was a risky pick for any team choosing at the number two spot when other talents such as Michael Jordan, Sam Perkins, and Charles Barkley were still available.

However, Portland general manager Stu Inman was steadfast in his belief that they needed to draft Sam Bowie. They did so and decided to pass on the most talented player in the entire draft class—Michael Jordan. In the modern-day NBA, any general manager would draft the most talented player available instead of looking for someone who could fit the team personnel and system. After all, it would be easier to work for a trade for someone talented and healthy instead of running the risk of drafting someone who might not stay healthy.

With the Blazers' decision to take Bowie with the second overall pick, the entire field was open for the Chicago Bulls, owner of the third overall pick, to take the most talented player in that draft class. It was a simple choice to make when they took Michael Jordan out of North Carolina because there was no other player who had the combination of his athletic prowess and skill level.

What the Chicago Bulls had in Michael Jordan was a young shooting guard who was similar to Julius Erving in size, build, and athletic capabilities. Even though Hakeem Olajuwon was a logical choice for the top overall pick in an era where big men were still the most important players of any team, the consensus was that Jordan had more talent and was more refined than any other player in that draft class. He was not only quick and athletic but was also capable enough as a ball-handler and shooter because of how he was able to refine his skills under Dean Smith's tutelage back in North Carolina. On top of that, it was an indisputable fact that Michael Jordan was already a defensive gem as early as his college years.

The Chicago Bulls knew what Michael Jordan was capable of when it came to offense and defense. However, what they did not know was that he had the competitive drive and the work ethic that would help turn him into the greatest player of all time. And even though the Portland Trailblazers' Stu Inman was aware of Jordan's talent, he still defended his choice of Bowie over Jordan until his death.[viii]

All of us probably know what Jordan turned out to be. However, Sam Bowie would ostensibly become the biggest bust in league history—not because he was not talented, not because he was injury-prone, but because he was taken before Michael Jordan. Bowie struggled to stay healthy throughout his NBA career due to the injuries he suffered back in college. Meanwhile, aside from Jordan, two other players from that draft class, Charles Barkley and John Stockton, became Hall of Famers. The fact that the Blazers missed out on all three of these incredible talents was probably their biggest mistake, but the jaw-dropping fact that they had a chance to take Jordan but didn't became the most notable—it was a faux pas for the ages that would alter the way most teams think about drafting in the years to come. And as history unfolded in the wake of Michael Jordan's career, that ill-fated draft choice became the ultimate story about "the one that got away."

And while we can talk about how things would have changed for both Michael Jordan and the Blazers had Portland decided to draft him, what is indisputable is that being in Chicago was what allowed Jordan to have a stage that elevated him to the same level as all of the other stars in the league at that time. It was time for Michael Jordan to soar high in the NBA.

The Birth of Air Jordan—Rookie of the Year

During the 1980s, the basketball sneaker culture was not as big as it is now. Players back then wore Converse shoes because that company was the biggest athletic shoe provider in all of basketball. They had the likes of Larry Bird, Magic Johnson, and Julius Erving, the three most popular players of the era, representing them. And, back then, basketball sneakers were "vanilla" in the sense that there were not a lot of differences between one pair of shoes and another.

Because Michael Jordan was a hot commodity out of North Carolina, where he had already made a name for himself as a popular high-flying wing, he was also going to be a pretty interesting choice for shoe companies to try to win over. Jordan and his agent were already shopping for shoe endorsements before he got to the NBA. And, at that time, MJ wanted to wear Adidas because he always dreamed of representing that rising company ever since he was in college.[ix]

Luck was not on Jordan's side, however, when they tried to pitch a deal with Adidas. The company was not in the best shape due to internal problems. They simply could not afford to bring in Michael Jordan, who was disappointed by the fact that he could not represent his dream shoe company. This made MJ's camp go to Converse.

Michael Jordan loved the fact that Converse wanted to treat him in a similar way as they did the NBA superstars that were already representing them. They were about to take the offer but James Jordan intervened. Mike's father asked Converse what kind of innovative design they had to offer to Jordan. As mentioned, Converse back then was a vanilla shoe company when it came to their basketball sneakers. Magic's shoe was not much different from Larry's. Wearing boring, unoriginal shoes would not have allowed Michael Jordan to stand out.

And on Converse's part, they were not willing to offer more to a rookie who was yet to play his first NBA game.

Nike then came in to try to win over Michael Jordan. Nike recognized Jordan's potential star power—he was already a household name after leading the 1984 Olympic USA Men's Basketball Team to a gold medal finish. The company was rising fast but they needed to be represented by that one big superstar to truly become a giant in the athletic shoe industry. At first, Michael Jordan did not even want to meet with Nike. Yet, he was convinced to go and meet with the company's representatives. That meeting changed the shoe industry as we know it.

Michael Jordan agreed to the Nike deal after he got an offer worth $500,000 for five years. At that time, that was a crazy sum for any athlete. However, Nike told Michael Jordan that the only way for his final two years of his deal to get guaranteed was for him to sell $4 million worth of shoes by the time he reached his third year in the NBA. What Nike did not know was that they had someone so special that it was going to be easy for him to sell his shoes. They went with the first Air Jordan sneakers that featured the classic Nike wings logo that is still very popular even to this day.

Wearing Air Jordan shoes, the true Air Jordan was able to showcase how he truly lived up to his name when he made his rookie debut with the Chicago Bulls. At that time, the Bulls and even the city of Chicago were in a drought in respect to sports talent. They did not have someone they could rely on to help unite the entire city in a sporting cause. At the time, most of their sports teams struggled to win games and even sell tickets. The Chicago Bulls, during the 1983-84 season, only won 27 games and were third to last in terms of attendance. Their best player was Orlando Woolridge, an effective scorer at the forward position and a good slam-dunker, but he just did not have that "it" factor.

Michael Jordan, on the other hand, was poised to help electrify the city of Chicago. He may not have had the best debut when he went for 16 points in a win against the Washington Bullets on October 26, 1984, but it did not take him long to adjust to the style of play in the NBA. It was on November 13th when he proved himself to be the next big thing in basketball. In a win over the San Antonio Spurs, Jordan finished with 45 points and 10 rebounds. He eventually averaged 25 points per game in his first 20 games in the NBA. Jordan was already scoring more points in the NBA than he did back when he was in college. And as the season progressed, he continued to get better and better.

Jordan had a triple-double performance of 35 points, 14 rebounds, and 15 assists on January 14, 1985, against the Denver Nuggets in a win. He would have two more triple-doubles during his rookie year as the entire NBA become witnesses to what the newest league sensation was capable of.

As Jordan's popularity rose, so did his fanbase. MJ was dominating the scoring end at such a high level for a rookie that he was able to gravitate fans towards him. On top of that, his highflying plays and impossible finishes made him an instant sensation. The league simply had never seen a player like Jordan. Dr. J was the closest but, at that early juncture in his career, Mike was already demonstrating skills and talents that not even Julius Erving had. It was as if he had taken what his predecessor had and made it into something unique to his image and playing style.

With his highflying performances and exploding popularity, Michael Jordan was a marketing gem for his Air Jordan shoes. At that time, the league was unhappy with Jordan's Nike sneakers and actually banned them—not because they gave him an unfair advantage but because they did not fit the league's policies on shoe colors. Nike suffered no ill effects from this ban, however. Instead, they turned it into an opportunity to market their shoes by making fans believe that wearing them gave them a competitive advantage. As innovative as the Air Jordans already were, they were not very different from other sneakers on the market. But thanks to Nike's clever marketing strategy, kids started wanting to be "like Mike" by wearing them.

As a result, sales went through the roof. From the targeted $4 million worth of Air Jordan shoes that Nike was planning on selling, Michael Jordan's popularity and ability to play an entirely different brand of basketball made him the biggest shoe seller in the entire basketball playing field. Just a year after signing his contract with Nike, Michael

Jordan sold $100 million worth of shoes—25 times more than what they were originally planning to sell.

Michael Jordan's contribution to the rise of athletic shoe culture was immeasurable. After his rookie year, he continued to release newer variants of the Air Jordan line of sneakers until Jordan became a brand entirely on its own under Nike. To this date, Jordan sneakers are still the most popular shoes on the market. The athletic shoe market is far different now than it was in the 1980s as companies have focused on technological innovations that improved shoe performance. This was all thanks to how Michael Jordan's Air Jordans changed the way we look at basketball sneaker culture. His influence single-handedly and irrevocably changed the industry.

With Michael Jordan's rise to popularity, it was impossible for fans to not vote for him as an All-Star. In fact, he was only third behind Moses Malone and Isiah Thomas in votes in the Eastern Conference All-Stars. Jordan garnered more votes than established stars such as Larry Bird and Julius Erving. However, controversy was quick to strike during the All-Star festivities.

Word quickly spread that Michael Jordan was becoming more popular than any other player while garnering attention that no rookie has ever had in the history of the NBA. Allegations came out that the Detroit Pistons point guard Isiah Thomas planned on "freezing" him out of the game by preventing him from getting any possessions for himself.[x] As such, Michael Jordan only ended up with 7 points on 9 shots in that game. This alleged "freeze out" led by Thomas was the earliest stage of what would become a personal rivalry and feud between Jordan and the Pistons' all-time great point guard. The East ended up losing that game to the West as Houston's Ralph Sampson ended up with the All-Star MVP Award. Things might have changed had Jordan been able to play normally in that game.

But, even though Michael Jordan was becoming a cultural icon on his own while also changing the culture in Chicago, things were not as easy as they were during his rookie year. Prior to his arrival, the Bulls overall mindset was not entirely suited for competitive basketball. Players were more inclined towards having fun and partying than on working on their individual skills. One instance was when, during one of their road games, Michael Jordan saw practically the entire team in one single room doing drugs. He got invited to join in but declined. Jordan cared more about his future than having the worst kind of fun a young star could ever have. MJ said that he was more interested in playing hard and working on his game than on doing drugs.[xi]

From what Jordan once described as a "traveling cocaine circus," the Bulls eventually changed its culture to fit the kind of player that Mike was. He needed to be surrounded by players who not only complemented his style of play but were also as hungry as he was to win games. Not many of those teammates ended up staying long with the Bulls shortly after Chicago acquired Michael Jordan, as they steadily unloaded the roster and acquired different pieces that could complement their best player's gifts.

Michael Jordan averaged 28.2 points, 6.5 rebounds, 5.9 assists, and 2.4 steals as a rookie. His scoring average was the highest for a rookie since Kareem Abdul-Jabbar averaged nearly 29 points in his rookie season. With shooting percentages of 51.5% from the field and 84.5% from the free-throw line, he also proved himself to be an efficient scorer. Jordan took the NBA by storm and led the team to 38 wins and a playoff berth in only his first season with the Chicago Bulls. However, they lost to the Milwaukee Bucks in only four games in the first round of the postseason.

The Injury Year

There was no doubt in anyone's mind that Michael Jordan was still on the rise. Though the rookie year was often the peak for a lot of star players, MJ's talent and natural athletic gifts were still improving. He was sure to become even better than what he showed during his rookie year. But, unfortunately, time would reveal that not even the best and most talented player of all time was safe from injury.

In just his third game of the regular season, Michael Jordan suffered a broken foot that required him to miss a total of 64 games that season until his eventual return in the middle of March 1986. Despite Jordan's prolonged absence, he still managed to get voted in as an All-Star starter due to how immensely popular he already was. Needless to say, he missed his second All-Star season due to his injury.

Even though Michael Jordan was able to return to the lineup on March 15, 1986, there were still a lot of risks involved when he came back. Doctors were unsure if he should have forced himself to return to the game, but Jordan, a player on the rise, was not going to let the injury hamper his development as an NBA superstar.

When he was trying to get back to full form, Michael Jordan learned from his doctors that forcing his way back to what he was before the injury had a lot of risks involved. He revealed in the documentary *The Last Dance* that there was a 10% chance that he would end up aggravating the injury and ending his career as a result. As defiant as he was, Jordan said that he was willing to take the risk and play through the injury because he still had a 90% chance that he would not end up aggravating his broken foot. He was willing to risk his entire career for a chance to return to the floor and help push his Bulls forward.

Michael Jordan, however, eventually agreed to concede to his doctor's advice somewhat when Bulls' owner Jerry Reinsdorf told him that the risk-to-reward ratio was not in his favor if he forced himself to play at a stellar level that season. The Bulls may have been in a position to reach the playoffs but they were not going to go deep with the roster that they had that year. That considered, there really was no reason for Jordan to force himself back at full steam.

On March 15th, Michael Jordan returned to the lineup but under the condition that he would be under a strict minutes restriction. It did not matter whether or not he was hot or if the Bulls needed him to be on the floor to win games. What mattered most was for them to preserve their franchise star's health and to make sure that he would be able to get back to full health on a long-term basis. There were instances where the Bulls needed to win games on a single basket but the coaching staff still did not put Jordan on the floor no matter how much they may have wanted to.

It was only during April when Michael Jordan began playing 30 minutes a night again because of how well his injury was improving. However, MJ still did not force himself too much because he understood that they needed him to be at full health when the playoffs began. As such, he went on to average only 22.7 points during that season while starting only seven games. Four-time scoring champion George "The Iceman" Gervin, who was in his final year in the NBA, and capable forward Orlando Woolridge, carried the Chicago Bulls to 30 wins as they barely made the playoffs.

As quiet as Michael Jordan was during the regular season as he was recuperating from his injury, he was allowed to let himself loose during the playoffs and to release all of his pent-up frustrations on the Boston Celtics, a 67-win team with the MVP Larry Bird leading a group of All-Stars. It was the Big Three era of the Celtics at their prime playing against a rising Michael Jordan, who was on his way to take the best player crown away from Larry Bird.

With virtually no help in Game 1 of their series against the Celtics, Michael Jordan introduced himself to his stellar opponents by igniting them for 49 big points. However, he was just one superstar against a team that was constructed to win it all that season. There was no way Jordan was going to win against such odds regardless of how phenomenal he was.

Before Game 2 of that series, Michael Jordan actually played golf with the Celtics' starting shooting guard, Danny Ainge. Jordan was always a fan of golf and was fond of playing that sport whenever he was free. Even though golf was just a hobby for him, his competitive spirit was still at the highest level. Ainge was talking trash to him the entire game. And after the end of their match, Jordan told Ainge that he had something special for them the next game.

True enough, Michael Jordan was a one-man wrecking crew in what was one of the fiercest playoff games ever played during that era. With Jordan making sure that he was competing the entire game against a team full of stars, he never let up and forced the Celtics' backs up against the wall in a double-overtime classic.

No matter what kind of defense the Celtics gave him, Jordan was getting to his spots and was hitting his shots over multiple defenders. At the end of what was a losing effort for him, MJ tallied 63 points on a 22-out-of-41 shooting clip. That scoring performance remains the highest scoring mark a player has ever achieved in the playoffs. And, even though the Bulls lost that game, Michael Jordan received the highest praise any player could ever get when the MVP Larry Bird, who did not typically give out compliments to his opponents, said that they just went up against "God disguised as Michael Jordan".[xii] At that moment, even Bird was acknowledging that Jordan was at an entirely different level as an individual player.

The Boston Celtics figured Michael Jordan out in Game 3 as the rising superstar finally ran out of gas. He only had 19 points as the Chicago Bulls bowed out of the playoffs in only three games against a 67-win Boston Celtics squad. Larry Bird and the entire Celtics squad eventually won the NBA championship that season against the Houston Rockets and Hakeem Olajuwon, who was able to make it to the Finals long before Jordan did.

The One-Man Show, Falling to the Pistons

With Michael Jordan's rise as a bona fide superstar after that stellar series against the Boston Celtics, the Chicago Bulls realized that they needed to build around him by surrounding their franchise player with a supporting cast that could make things easier for him. Meanwhile, new head coach Doug Collins, at the tender age of 35 years old, wanted to unleash Michael Jordan and make full use of his best player's otherworldly capabilities on the floor. Stat-wise, it was under Collins that Jordan was able to put up the best statistical seasons of his career.

Michael Jordan did not waste any time at the start of the 1986-87 season when the greatest individual player of that generation put up

50

50 points against the New York Knicks in his season debut on November 1, 1986. That performance was not a fluke as Jordan went on to have 16 games of scoring 40 or more points in his first 25 games during the regular season. At one point, he even had nine straight games of scoring at least 40 points.

On January 8, 1987, Michael Jordan put up a new season-high of 53 points in a win over the Portland Trailblazers. Performances such as those solidified his claim to the top spot of the entire NBA when it came to who was the best player in the entire league as far as individual talents go. And because of his popularity, Jordan went on to lead the entire NBA in All-Star votes that season.

Michael Jordan set another season-high in points when he had 58 points against the New Jersey Nets on February 26th. He needed to shoot only 25 attempts from the floor due to how much the Nets fouled him. Jordan made 26 of his 27 foul shots in that game. It did not take long for MJ to surpass himself yet again when he notched a regular-season career-high of 61 points against the Detroit Pistons on March 4th.

Near the end of the season, Michael Jordan had one of the greatest three-game runs a player could ever have. He had 53 points against the Indiana Pacers on March 12th before going for 50 against the Milwaukee Bucks just a night later. He then capped off his three-game run by proving that he was better than Dominique Wilkins when he scored 61 points against the Atlanta Hawks on March 16th. During that run, Jordan averaged 54.7 points, 7.7 rebounds, 4 steals, and 2 blocks.

At the end of the regular season, Michael Jordan enjoyed one of the best statistical seasons a player could ever have; he was the first player since Wilt Chamberlain to score 3,000 in a single season. He averaged 37.1 points, 5.2 rebounds, 4.6 assists, 2.9 steals, and 1.5 blocks. No other player since then has been able to put up 3,000 points while averaging at least 37 points in a single season. Similarly, Michael Jordan also became the first player in league history to have 200 steals and 100 blocks in a single season to prove that he was not only an offensive juggernaut but also a defensive force as well.

But, despite how gaudy Michael Jordan's numbers were, the MVP Award went to the Los Angeles Lakers' Magic Johnson, who averaged 24 points and more than 12 assists while leading his team to 65 wins that season. As history would show, the MVP Award has always been awarded to a player with the best combination of stats and wins. On his part, Jordan was only able to lead his Bulls to 40 wins that season.

Just like the previous year, Michael Jordan went up against the Boston Celtics in the first round of the playoffs. This time, however, there were no godlike performances on Jordan's part, even though he still put up pretty good numbers in that series. The Celtics were just too good while the Bulls were still only a team relying on a single superstar. The series ended in favor of Boston in only three games yet again.

Losing in the first round of the playoffs for three straight seasons meant that not even Michael Jordan was capable enough to lead a team full of role players without the right complementary help and the right system that could bring out the best in him. We have all seen a lot of insanely capable individual players in the history of the NBA but none of them were able to win titles until they started playing together with players that complemented their capabilities. That was what Jordan needed in his fourth season. And that was why team executive Jerry Krause filled that need during the 1987 NBA Draft.

The Chicago Bulls owned the eighth and tenth pick of that year's draft following trades done since acquiring Michael Jordan. Krause brought a wing named Scottie Pippen for a workout and was astonished by what the young 6'8" forward could do as far as his physical capabilities were concerned. Pippen might not have had the same skillset as Michael Jordan but he was every bit the athlete that MJ was. And what really impressed Krause was Pippen's lateral movement—a hallmark of what makes a great defensive player in the NBA. Both the Bulls' owner and the executives agreed that they needed to trade up for Pippen because they were unsure about his availability at the eighth pick.[xiii]

True enough, Chicago was able to make a move that allowed them to move up to the fifth spot of the draft when they made a deal with the

Seattle SuperSonics, who went on to draft Pippen for them and traded him to the Bulls. And, at the tenth pick of the draft, Chicago chose capable power forward Horace Grant. While both Pippen and Grant were yet to contribute significantly during their rookie seasons in the NBA, they were the two most important pieces in what would become the first basketball dynasty in Chicago under Michael Jordan's leadership.

Jordan might have acquired new, talented teammates but they were merely rookies who were still improving and learning how to play the NBA game. It was still up to MJ to carry the team on his shoulders during the 1987-88 season. Even though he did not have the same hot start that he had a season ago, Jordan was still able to go for 40 or more points five times in his first 25 games. The highlight of that good start was on December 17, 1987, when he finished a win over the Cleveland Cavaliers with 52 big points.

Evolving as a great defensive player, Michael Jordan was also making a name for himself as arguably the most well-rounded defender in the league. One example of his great defensive instincts was when he had 10 steals and 2 blocks while scoring 32 points in only 27 minutes of play against the New Jersey Nets on January 29, 1988. But scoring was still his top priority as he went on to average 33.5 points at that juncture of the season. Needless to say, he was once again the most popular player come All-Star weekend.

The 1988 Slam Dunk Contest was one of the highlights of the 1988 All-Star festivities. This featured a competitive display of dunks between the night's two best dunkers, Michael Jordan and "The Human Highlight Film," Dominique Wilkins. Defending his Slam Dunk title, Michael Jordan went for the most iconic dunk of his life when he made his signature dunk from the free-throw line to win the event. It was the image of this electrifying free-throw line dunk that ultimately became the logo of his Jordan brand under Nike. After winning the Slam Dunk Contest for a second straight season, MJ competed in the All-Star Game and won it for the Eastern Conference All-Stars as the MVP.

Michael Jordan upped his individual performances after the All-Star break and went on to average 36.6 points in the final 37 games of the regular season. During that span of games, he scored 40 or more points 10 times while scoring 50 or more points in three of those games. His season-high in points came on April 3, 1988, when he had 59 points on a majestic shooting line of 21 out of 27 from the field against the Detroit Pistons in a win.

At the end of the regular season, Michael Jordan averaged 35 points, 5.5 rebounds, 5.9 assists, 3.2 steals, and 1.6 blocks. He led the league in scoring once again and finished as the league leader in steals as well. Jordan also improved his shooting percentage to 53.5% after shooting under 50% a year ago. In fact, statistically, this was Michael Jordan's finest and most efficient season as far as the numbers and overall efficiency were concerned, even though he did not have the same kind of scoring year that he had in the previous season.

Jordan led the Chicago Bulls to a 50-win season, which was their best since the NBA and ABA merged in 1976. For his astounding leadership in helping the Bulls rise up while putting up tremendous stats the world has not seen in more than two decades, Michael Jordan was named the league MVP over both Magic Johnson and Larry Bird, cementing his place as the league's newest top dog when it came to what he could do at an individual level.

Michael Jordan was also named the league's Defensive Player of the Year and became the first player to win MVP and DPOY in the same year. Hakeem Olajuwon would become the only other player to do that. Michael Jordan did not only establish his place as the top offensive player but he also made it a point to make it known to the world that he was also the league's best perimeter defender.

In the first round of the playoffs that season, Michael Jordan was at his absolute best as he was trying to win his first-ever playoff series and finally make it out of the first round. The Cleveland Cavaliers were tough to beat that year, especially with the well-rounded offense they played. But Jordan was an offensive machine on his own throughout the entire series. He scored 50 and 55 points respectively in Games 1 and 2, which were both wins. And while the Cavs won the next two games, Jordan scored 39 in Game 5 to push the Bulls past the first round for the first time under his leadership. The MVP averaged 45.2 points during the entire series.

Defensively, the Cavaliers had no game plan that could stop Michael Jordan. But the Detroit Pistons, the Chicago Bulls' second-round opponents, were entirely different. That group of players, led by Jordan's archnemesis Isiah Thomas, may not have had a lot of capable stars, however, they all complemented one another on the defensive end. Joe Dumars and Dennis Rodman were the designated "Jordan stoppers" out on the perimeter. And if MJ was capable enough to get past his main defenders, the paint was going to be an even greater challenge.

The trademark defense that made the 1980s Detroit Pistons such a dangerous team was their physicality inside the paint. During an era where players were basically allowed to clobber each other down in the middle without getting called for excessive contact, the Pistons were able to do whatever they wanted to any star player that dared to try to score in the paint.

While other teams contested and blocked shots, the Pistons hit players hard to deter them from scoring in the paint. It helped that they had a collection of physical frontline players that made it possible for them to stop the likes of Michael Jordan. Bill Laimbeer led Rick Mahorn, Dennis Rodman, and John Salley, none of whom were afraid of dropping people to the ground with their physical inside defense. That was why the 1980s Pistons were called the "Bad Boys."

Detroit's physical play was on full display against Michael Jordan in their first encounter in the playoffs in 1988. This was when Jordan's Pistons demons started to surface as Detroit's head coach, Chuck Daly, made use of the allowable physicality to develop a defensive strategy more commonly known as "the Jordan rules."[xiv]

Their defensive philosophy against Jordan involved influencing him to the elbow to prevent him from going baseline. As much as possible, they were also going to stop him from going right and from taking his defenders down in the low post by trapping him. And when he did find a way to drive baseline, that was when the Pistons frontline would clobber him to the ground and basically hurt him.

The key here was that the Bad Boys were going to deter Jordan from dunking on the team or from scoring inside the paint. He needed to beat them from the perimeter. And if he could not score from the perimeter due to how the Pistons were trapping him, he had to pass the ball out to his teammates. Detroit was willing to gamble on the rest of the Bulls to try to beat them. It was a good gamble because no one other than Jordan was capable of putting up 20 points.

Detroit's Jordan Rules worked. They were able to contain the MVP and the greatest individual player in the world to only 27.4 points during the entire series. Chicago only won one game, and that was when MJ had his best shooting and scoring night. However, the Bulls ended up losing in five games to the Pistons as Detroit proved that

Chicago could not amount to anything when the best player in the world was struggling to score.

The following season saw some improvements in that regard, however. Both Scottie Pippen and Horace Grant were able to improve after spending a year as role players for the Chicago Bulls. It was also during the 1988-89 season when Jordan once again had one of the most fantastic statistical seasons an individual could ever have just a year after putting up his most efficient season as a pro.

During the early period of the new season, Michael Jordan scored 52 points three times in a span of nine games. He did so against the Boston Celtics, the Philadelphia 76ers, and the Denver Nuggets. However, it was later on January 21, 1989, when he outdid his scoring high that season by going for 53 points and 14 rebounds in a loss to the Phoenix Suns.

During the latter part of the 1988-89 season, head coach Doug Collins started tinkering around with the lineup by placing Michael Jordan at the point guard spot. That was when Michael Jordan showcased his array of playmaking skills by focusing more on getting his teammates involved instead of looking for his own shot. In the final 27 games of the regular season, Jordan had a total of 12 triple-doubles. At one point, he had seven straight triple-doubles. He also had a high of 17 assists in one of those 27 games. During the time when he was playing point guard, he was putting up 30 points, 9 rebounds, and more than 10 assists.

When the regular season ended, Michael Jordan averaged 32.5 points and career-highs of 8 rebounds and 8 assists per game. As a point guard during the latter part of the season, he was asked to make plays for his teammates. And, because the team lost Charles Oakley during the offseason, Jordan was also rebounding more at that time. That was why he ended the season with a total of 15 triple-doubles while becoming the first player since 1965 to post a 30-8-8 season. The last player to do that was Oscar Robertson.

The next time a player accomplished this feat came later on in 2017 when Russell Westbrook averaged a 30-point triple-double. This goes to show how well-rounded a player Jordan was back in the 1980s when the pace was not yet as fast as it was during the late 2010s. Had he played point guard earlier that season, or had he played in today's era, he may have also averaged a triple-double himself.

It was Magic Johnson who ended up winning the MVP Award that season in what was one of the closest MVP races of that era. Jordan may have had the stats but it was Magic who ended up with a better team. The Lakers won 57 games during the regular season. Meanwhile, the Chicago Bulls once again struggled to get to the playoffs after winning only 47 games.

The Chicago Bulls secured another first-round date against the Cleveland Cavaliers. At that time, there was no arguing the fact that the Cavs had a better and more well-rounded team than the Bulls. They won 57 regular-season games and had four players averaging at least 17 points. Their balanced attack included three All-Stars, namely hot-shooting point guard Mark Price, high-flying Larry Nance, and Jordan's former North Carolina teammate, Brad Daugherty.

Even though the Cavaliers sported a better team and a more balanced attack, what they did not factor in was the fact that they still did not have any idea how to stop Michael Jordan, who tore them up for 44 points in Game 3 and 50 points in Game 4. However, as excellent a series as it was for Jordan, the Cavs still forced Game 5 after winning Game 4 when Jordan fouled out. It was that Game 4 loss that opened the gates to one of Michael Jordan's most iconic moments.

Game 5 was a tight one but Michael Jordan was countering every punch that the Cavaliers were giving the Bulls. MJ ended up giving the Bulls a 99-98 lead during the final moments of the game when he drained a tough shot over the bigger Larry Nance. However, the Cavaliers went on to think they had the victory in the bag when role player Craig Ehlo hit a layup with only three seconds left on the clock. At that moment, everyone in Cleveland thought they were going to win the game and eliminate the Bulls in five games.

The Bulls had a timeout and Doug Collins decided to call a play that would have center David Corzine hitting the game-winner because the coach was trying to go for something that was not obvious. Michael Jordan basically vetoed that play and just told his coach to give him the ball. Meanwhile, on the other end, the Cavs' head coach, Lenny Wilkens, who was one of the most decorated coaches in league history, probably made a crucial mistake when he was drawing up the defensive play.

Lenny Wilkens asked Craig Ehlo to defend Jordan in that final play instead of giving the defensive duties to the better defender, Ron Harper, who would later become the Bulls designated point guard stopper during the late 1990s. Jordan later said in *The Last Dance* that putting Ehlo on him was a mistake because he thought that Ron Harper was doing a better defensive job on him.[xv]

As the play was about to commence, Michael Jordan started from the top of the key below the three-point line, fought his way through defenders to receive the ball just above the right wing three-point line. The moment he got the ball, he dribbled left just about two feet above the free-throw line, rose up for a shot, and hung in the air for what seemed like an eternity.

During that play, it was Craig Ehlo defending the greatest player in the world. As a role player, that game was supposed to be his moment. He scored 24 points that night and went on to contribute 15 points in the final quarter alone. Ehlo was also one of the key figures in the final three plays of that game. The first one was when Jordan was able to drive past him to hit a tough shot over Larry Nance to give the Bulls the lead with six seconds. Upon closer inspection, the reason why MJ was able to easily drive past Ehlo was that he got inadvertently hit on the face by Jordan's elbow while the latter began his motion for the drive. However, Ehlo thought he redeemed himself by hitting a tough layup over multiple Bulls defenders including Michael Jordan with three seconds left.

But, while Ehlo thought he was about to have a moment that would define his career as a role player, it was the opposite. The moment Jordan received the ball with three seconds left, he got half a step on the slower Ehlo. He may have recovered at the right moment when Jordan was already up in the air as he contested the shot in the best way he could. Against any other player, that contest by Ehlo was an excellent one and may have prevented a good look.

However, Michael Jordan was an entirely different breed. When he rose up in the air as Ehlo was still recovering, he had all the space he needed. Ehlo may have recovered in time to contest his shot, but Jordan used every bit of athleticism he had in his legs to rise up high just so he could have a fraction of a second left for him to get a good shot after his defender flew by. MJ hung in the air long enough to release a shot before landing. And, as focused as he was at that moment in time, Michael Jordan hit the shot as Craig Ehlo crumbled down to the floor, knowing that he had been robbed of his moment. That shot by Michael Jordan would later be called "The Shot."

In that series against the Cavs, Michael Jordan averaged 39.8 points, 5.8 rebounds, and 8.2 assists. He finished Game 5 with 44 points after hitting The Shot. In the second round, he also got past the Knicks, who were also a better team than the Bulls. Jordan averaged 35.7 points, 9.5 rebounds, and 8.3 assists against New York. He had a triple-double of 34 points, 10 rebounds, and 12 assists in Game 1. The Bulls won against the Knicks in six games.

Michael Jordan once again met the Detroit Pistons in the playoffs. This time, however, it was for a chance to play in the NBA Finals. Jordan, at first, thought that he had figured out the Pistons' Jordan Rules when the Bulls won Games 1 and 3 to go up 2-1 in the series. MJ had 32 points in Game 1 before going for 46 points in Game 3. But the Pistons recovered and figured out once again how to stop the greatest player in the NBA. They clobbered him in Games 4 and 5 while limiting him to a total of only 23 shots in those two games. He only had eight shots in Game 5. Finally, in Game 6, Detroit put the Bulls to rest and made it all the way to the NBA Finals where they swept the previously undefeated Los Angeles Lakers to win the franchise's first NBA championship.

For another season, Michael Jordan was once again the king without a crown. He may have been the best player in the NBA but he could not cement his claim to that accolade if he did not have a championship under his belt. At that time, Magic Johnson and Larry Bird were already multiple-time champions and already had nothing left to prove in their careers. Even Jordan's rival, Isiah Thomas, was already a champion after the Pistons essentially became the new team to beat when they defeated Bird's Boston Celtics and Johnson's Los Angeles Lakers in the same year to win the title.

However, neither Mike nor the Bulls knew how to solve the issues surrounding their inability to defeat the Bad Boys era of the Detroit Pistons. If they wanted to secure their spot at the top of the NBA, they had to go through Detroit. But, because things were not working, the Chicago Bulls decided to make some drastic changes heading into the 1989-90 season.

After three seasons as the head coach of the Chicago Bulls, Doug Collins was fired from his position. Under Collins, Michael Jordan was unleashed and had the best three statistical seasons of his career, primarily because his head coach built a team that focused on him alone, while the other players on the roster were simply there to play off of him. As such, the Pistons figured out the formula when they noticed that Chicago struggled to win when Jordan was pushed out of the picture.

As much as Michael Jordan loved Doug Collins, the Bulls front office did not think that going with him was the best choice heading forward. Tex Winter, who Jerry Krause described as "the finest offensive mind in basketball," was an assistant with the Bulls and was in charge of drawing up different offensive sets.[xvi] However, it was revealed in *The Last Dance* that Collins did not exactly agree with Winter's offensive philosophies and even went on to remove him from the coaching staff's bench during games.

But when the front office fired Collins and replaced him with former Bulls' assistant coach Phil Jackson, Tex Winter was finally able to sell his offense to the new head coach. Jackson was always someone who tried to think outside the box. A former NBA champion himself while playing for the New York Knicks during the early 1970s, Phil Jackson went on to have a successful career coaching overseas. And being someone who loved thinking well beyond the norm, he used to sympathize with the counterculture when he was still playing in the NBA. He was the perfect man to institute the triangle offense, an offensive system developed and perfected by Tex Winter himself.

Not many people understand what the triangle offense is all about. It is essentially a system wherein a post player anchors the offense on the block while a guard waits out in the corner and a swingman stands by in the wing. These three points form a triangle that opens up a lot of options for the offense. The post player has the option of scoring down in the low block or passing out to the perimeter players who form the other two points of the triangle. Meanwhile, the other guard waits out at the top of the three-point line and the other forward flashes to the opposite side of the top of the key as a backup option in case the defense commits to the triangle.

The main purpose of the triangle offense is to allow the players to open up their options without having to rely on one key playmaker to do all the passing for them. This essentially involves ball movement and knowing how to read where the defense reacts to know where to pass the ball. Jackson and Winters instituted this offense for the Bulls primarily to help find a back door to the Jordan Rules defense of the Detroit Pistons. So, instead of running the offense through Jordan as the primary scorer and playmaker, the Chicago Bulls would now have multiple offensive options and playmakers because of the triangle offense.

At first, Michael Jordan did not like the idea of using the triangle offense. He wanted the ball in his hands most of the time so that he could either create opportunities for himself or pass out to an open teammate when the defense collapsed down on him. But, most of all, he said in *The Last Dance* that he did not want the ball in the hands of a less-than-capable offensive player in the dire moments of a game just because the triangle offense demands the ball go through the hands of the different players that form the points of the triangle.[xvii]

Because of these reservations, Michael Jordan was not a huge fan of Phil Jackson when he first took the coaching helm from Doug Collins. He made it clear that he did not like the fact that Jackson did not want Jordan to hold onto the ball for 99% of the time. However, Phil Jackson addressed his superstar's concern early on and made him understand the purpose of the triangle offense.

Jackson said that, in any kind of offensive system, the focus of the defense is on the ball and not on the superstar. So, if the team's superstar did not have the ball in his hands, the opposing defense would most likely take their eyes off of him. However, if the superstar has the ball in his hands all the time, it will be easier for opposing defenses to formulate a plan that could counter that kind of an offense by simply taking away scoring opportunities from him. That was what the Pistons did to Jordan.

As a final note, Phil Jackson told Michael Jordan that he was not worried about him because he knew how talented he was. Anyone with Jordan's talent and skill level will shine no matter what kind of offense is being played. However, Jackson told Mike that what he *was* worried about was how to make his teammates better and how to create different threats that could pull defenses away from Jordan and towards the other guys on the team. It was this philosophy that ultimately sold Michael Jordan on the triangle offense.[xviii] Of course, the fact that the Bulls started winning more games helped to convince him as well.

Michael Jordan and the rest of the Chicago Bulls may have needed some time to adjust to the triangle offense, but the greatest player in the world was still up to his old tricks as the main scoring threat of the team. In just his first game under Phil Jackson, MJ scored 54 points in a win against the Cleveland Cavaliers.

However, over the course of the next two months, it was evident that the Bulls were passing and moving the ball around more than they did a year ago. Jordan shared the sugar and only had six games of scoring 40 or more points during the first two months of the 1989-90 season. His other 50-point game during those two months came in a loss to the newly formed Orlando Magic on December 20, 1989. He finished that game with 52 points.

While Michael Jordan still maintained his grip on the league's top-scoring plum that season, it was on March 28, 1990, that he had his finest individual performance during the regular season. In that win over the Cleveland Cavaliers, he proved that he had mastered their rival's defense over him by going for a career-high 69 points on top of collecting 18 rebounds. And he was not even done because he went on to score 49 and 47 in the next two games. The Bulls were in the middle of a nine-game winning streak at that time.

At the end of the regular season, Michael Jordan still led the league in scoring even though Phil Jackson was not expecting him to do so because of the triangle offense. He averaged 33.6 points, 6.9 rebounds, 6.3 assists, and 2.8 steals. But because Jordan did not have the ball in his hands all the time, his other teammates were allowed to flourish as well. The most notable of them was the third-year forward and new Bulls All-Star Scottie Pippen, whose numbers improved so much that he became a secondary scorer and playmaker behind Jordan. Pippen also alleviated a lot of defensive pressure from Jordan's shoulders as he was tasked with becoming the primary defender of the opposing team's best perimeter players.

In what was one of the tightest three-way finishes in MVP voting, Michael Jordan finished third behind Magic Johnson and Charles Barkley for the MVP Award, even though he had better stats and win shares than both of them. Nevertheless, Johnson rightfully won the award by virtue of the fact that he led the Los Angeles Lakers to 63 wins. Meanwhile, Jordan led the Bulls to a 55-win season, the highest win total they had had at that point since the NBA-ABA merger.

The Chicago Bulls managed to get through the first two rounds of the playoffs quite easily. They only lost one game each to the Milwaukee Bucks in the first round and to the Philadelphia 76ers in the second round. Through those two rounds, Michael Jordan averaged 40.2 points, 7.2 rebounds, 7.2 assists, and 3.3 steals. He was in prime shape heading into another fierce battle with the Detroit Pistons in the Conference Finals.

When the Detroit Pistons defeated the Bulls in the first two games while limiting Michael Jordan in those outings, it seemed as if Chicago was yet to solve the challenges of their Jordan Rules. But, when the series shifted over to Chicago for Games 3 and 4, MJ scorched them for a total of 89 points in those two games to tie the series at one game each. They would then trade blows in Games 5 and 6 to make way for a pivotal Game 7.

But, in Game 7, the Detroit Pistons' championship experience and solidarity won out when they defeated the Chicago Bulls by 19 points. Jordan had himself a good game after finishing with 31 points, 8 rebounds, and 9 assists. But, his efforts were not enough. The Chicago Bulls were still adjusting to the new offense while their two stars were developing. But, if there was anything they could take away from that loss to the Pistons during the 1990 playoffs, it was that they could beat them. Meanwhile, Detroit went on to win back-to-back NBA titles when they defeated Clyde Drexler's Portland Trailblazers in the Finals in five games.

The Rise of a Dynasty

The fact that Michael Jordan and the Chicago Bulls were potentially capable of beating the Detroit Pistons in a seven-game series under the new system and the new coaching staff gave the team renewed focus. And with a supporting cast led by Scottie Pippen, who was still improving every season, there were a lot of reasons for the Bulls faithful to feel optimistic about their chances during the 1990-91 season as the NBA bid farewell to the 1980s and said hello to the slower-paced, grind-it-out play style that was evolving as they headed into the 1990s.

But, for Michael Jordan to not only succeed during a physical 90s decade or even get through the Detroit Pistons in the playoffs, he still needed to grow—not only in terms of his skill level but also from a physical aspect. The Pistons spent three straight years beating him up and punishing him inside the paint. Jordan wanted none of that anymore. He wanted to be the one administering the pain. He wanted to be able to withstand that extreme physicality, not only from the Detroit Pistons but from other teams as well.

Up to that point in his career, Michael Jordan had tried his best to stay away from weights. He was always a fit but lean athlete, and he did not have the muscle weight and the strength that allowed him to punish opposing defenders or take the punishment himself. Avoiding

71

weights through his first six seasons in the NBA did not help him either. In some circles, Jordan was even seen as skinny, but he had always been hesitant to put on added muscle weight for fear that doing so might affect his movement and his jump shot.[xix]

As revealed in *The Last* Dance, getting perpetually mauled by the Detroit Pistons was what ultimately convinced him to begin lifting weights. Jordan hired the services of personal trainer Tim Grover, whom he gave 30 days to try to convince him that his program would work. Grover made Jordan lift weights and add some muscle and strength to his frame, but only in increments, which was key to making sure that the best player in the world did not end up shocking his body and changing the way it moved. Adding weight in controlled increments also allowed Jordan to slowly adjust to the changes his body was seeing so that he would not need to drastically adjust the way he moved or the way he shot the ball.

It turned out that Michael Jordan loved Grover's program so much that he ended up sticking with the personal trainer for the remainder of his professional career. The feelings of admiration and appreciation were mutual, as Grover realized how hard a worker this competitive basketball player truly was. Michael Jordan always pushed past the extra mile—he was fiercely dedicated to getting stronger and better.

Throughout the summer prior to the 1990-91 season, Jordan incrementally added 15 pounds to his frame and grew from a lean and skinny 200-pound athlete to a strong and capable 215-pound man who could dish out and take punishments without feeling worn out.

Coincidentally, by working out with Grover, Michael Jordan also changed the way basketball players saw their individual training regimens.[xix] Before Michael Jordan started working out and lifting weights, basketball players almost never hired their own personal trainers and would typically stick with the training staff that they had with their team. The problem, however, was that a team's training staff often approached the physical training of players by looking at the bigger picture instead of coming up with workouts and programs that specifically catered to the needs and playing style of individual players.

By working with his own personal trainer, Michael Jordan was able to demonstrate how beneficial it could be for an athlete to train according to what his own body demands. In his case, Jordan trained to focus more on strengthening his core so that it would be easier for all of his muscles to produce more force without having to exert more effort when doing so. Furthermore, this was what allowed Michael Jordan to stay away from injuries throughout the rest of his career, a remarkable change after spending the early portion of his NBA life suffering from various injuries.[xix]

The simple truth that Michael Joran was willing to work so hard to get even better when, in fact, he was already considered the greatest player in the world at that time is a testament to how special he truly was. He was always the first to tell you that he still had a lot of room left to grow. And by training his body to get stronger before the 1990-91 season, it gave the entire world the impression that this man approached his craft maniacally and obsessively.

The results showed throughout the 1990-91 season. Chicago might have struggled to get out of the gate early on after starting the first 11 games 5-6, but they soon turned that around to dominate the East, punctuated with mini winning streaks that were powered by Michael Jordan's ferocious competitive spirit, newly powerful physique, and the rest of the Bulls' dedication to the triangle system. And what was also impressive was that Jordan started learning how to delegate. He was still the top offensive option in the entire NBA, but he gave more room and leeway for Scottie Pippen to take on the offensive load by acting as the team's primary ball-handler and playmaker on top of playing his role as the team's secondary option on offense.

To that end, Michael Jordan began to focus more on getting quality baskets and on making the right plays on both offense and defense instead of trying to do more than he should. This allowed him to become more efficient as he did not have to do everything all by himself. In turn, MJ had one of his more statistically efficient seasons and went on to shoot his best percentage from the floor throughout the entire season.

Meanwhile, the Chicago Bulls remained steady the entire season. At one point, they even won 11 straight games during a span of nearly a month. And throughout the entire calendar months of February and March, the Bulls only lost four games. There was reason to believe that the Chicago Bulls could come out with the best record in the Eastern Conference.

When the season ended, Michael Jordan averaged 31.5 points, 6 rebounds, 5.5 assists, and 2.7 steals. He shot a career-high of 53.9% from the field while playing an average of 37 minutes, which turned out to be the lowest minutes he ever played as a Chicago Bull, not counting his injury-plagued second season. Jordan also won his fifth scoring title to break a tie with former teammate George Gervin for the second spot in most scoring titles won by a single player. However, unlike the previous years, there were no massive 50- and 60-point performances from Michael Jordan during the 1990-91 season. The entire season was all about forging team balance and consistently contributing without needing to do too much.

Michael Jordan ended up leading the Chicago Bulls to what was then a franchise-record of 61 wins during the regular season. Since he was putting up massive stats while leading the Bulls to the best record in the East, he was aptly named the league's Most Valuable Player. This time, however, he dominated the votes and was only 19 first-place votes shy of becoming a unanimous MVP winner.

While Michael Jordan spent the first six years of his career laboring his way through the playoffs, it was entirely different for him during the 1991 postseason. The Bulls' amazing team play and their solid defense allowed them to sweep past the New York Knicks in the first round. In fact, they even won Game 1 by a blowout margin of 41 points.

Jordan and company managed to easily pass by rival and fellow 1984 draft classmate Charles Barkley's Philadelphia 76ers in the second round. They won the series handily in only five games with MJ averaging terrific numbers of 33.4 points, 8 rebounds, and 7.8 assists. In Game 5 of that series, he thoroughly outplayed Barkley by grabbing 19 rebounds, even though his rival was primarily known for his ability to rebound the ball.

The win against the Sixers in the second round allowed the Chicago Bulls to secure a date with the Detroit Pistons in the Eastern Conference Finals. While the Pistons may have been the two-time defending champions, they were in the final legs of their mini-dynasty. Age and the downside of playing a relentlessly physical brand of basketball had finally caught up with them as they only won 50 games during the regular season. But that did not mean that the Bulls were allowed to slack off.

After three straight seasons of suffering at the hands of the Detroit Pistons both physically and mentally, a stronger and more experienced Michael Jordan was finally able to exorcise his demons during the 1991 season. He had finally beaten Isiah Thomas and the Bad Boy Detroit Pistons. And he did so emphatically by winning in four games and by buying into the Bulls' system. Knowing that he was once again going to be targeted by the Jordan Rules, MJ only averaged 17.8 shot attempts the entire series and focused more on making quality shots on his way to averaging 29.8 points in that four-game sweep.

As Chicago was on its way to beat Detroit by 21 points in Game 4 of that series, one of the most controversial moments in professional sports happened as the Pistons simply walked off the court in the dying seconds of the game without even approaching the Bulls to congratulate them. It was a changing of the guard in the East, but the former guard was too reluctant to give his post to the new guard.

In *The Last Dance*, Isiah Thomas explained that the walk-off was initiated by Pistons center Bill Laimbeer, who encouraged the team to go straight into the locker room without congratulating the Bulls. For Thomas and the rest of the Pistons, what they did was unprofessional, but they thought it was the way things were done back then. In fact, there was a precedence for it—The Boston Celtics did the same thing to them back when the Pistons took the Eastern Conference crown from them in 1988. For Thomas, doing the same thing to the Bulls was some sort of tradition in the East. But when Michael Jordan heard this explanation, he did not buy a single word that Thomas said, as the personal rivalry between two of the best guards of the 1980s still lived on.[xx] To Jordan, it was a clear case of poor sportsmanship.

Michael Jordan would go on to lead the Chicago Bulls to the franchise's first appearance in the NBA Finals. Awaiting them were

Magic Johnson and the Los Angeles Lakers, arguably the best team of the 1980s era. It was time for Jordan to bid farewell to relics of a bygone decade by beating a formidable Lakers team. Coincidentally, that Lakers squad featured James Worthy and Sam Perkins, his two best teammates when he won the NCAA title back in 1982.

Throughout the entire NBA Finals, Michael Jordan went back to his old ways and just simply carried the team on his back. He also did his best Magic Johnson impression by going for double-digit assists in all but one of the games they played against the Lakers. The Chicago Bulls ended up losing Game 1, though Jordan had 36 points and 12 assists. However, they went on to win the next four games.

The highlight of the entire Finals came in Game 2 when Michael Jordan streaked down the lane, motioned for a one-handed dunk with his right hand, then suddenly switched the ball to his left hand to lay the ball into the hoop as he was on his way down. While there was no real reason for him to do that move because no one actually challenged the shot mid-air, Jordan revealed that he instinctively switched the ball to his left hand when he saw his former North Carolina teammate Sam Perkins inside the lane. It was this shot that became the signature move of the 1991 NBA Finals, which was Michael Jordan's first title win.

As the dust settled, Michael Jordan and the Bulls came out the winner of a Finals series that turned out to be Magic Johnson's final playoff series, as he retired after the 1990-91 season due to HIV. Meanwhile,

Jordan was an NBA champion for the first time in his career. MJ went on to have a Magic-like Finals series after averaging 31.2 points, 6.6 rebounds, and 11.4 assists to win his first title ring in a span of seven seasons. He was awarded the Finals MVP Award due to his terrific play all series long.

While many people would point to Jordan's switching layup as the most memorable image of his first NBA championship win, it was the fact that he broke down and cried while holding the Finals trophy that stuck out the most with his teammates. Teammate Will Perdue said that he had only seen two types of emotions in a figure as enigmatic and as competitive as Michael Jordan—anger and frustration. However, seeing Jordan crying and breaking down made them all realize that this man was still as human as any other.

Jordan had been keeping those feelings deep inside him for so long that a championship win finally made him release all of his pent-up emotions and just cry them all out. Yes, Jordan was still human, even after every incredible athletic feat he has done to get to the top of the NBA mountain. And the next thing he needed to do was maintain his place up there at the top.

Three-Peat, First Retirement

Whenever someone gets to the top of the mountain, people are primed to try to do whatever they can to push them off that peak. That was what happened to Michael Jordan and the Chicago Bulls the moment they won the NBA championship. Teams around the NBA began forming squadrons that they believed could compete against the Bulls. Case in point, the New York Knicks hired former Lakers head coach Pat Riley to construct a team that could possibly dethrone Michael Jordan. It was a veritable epidemic of "Jordan Rules."

But despite the focused efforts to try to take the spotlight away from Michael Jordan, the greatest player in the world continued to play at the highest level while helping his team to a hot start during the regular season. Early on, the Bulls seemed unbeatable as they only lost a handful of games during the 1991-92 season's first few months.

It was, of course, Michael Jordan who led the way for the Bulls, especially when he had three straight 40-point games at the start of the season. His season-high early on was when he had 46 points against the Milwaukee Bucks on November 2, 1991. He finished that mini-run with 44 points against the Boston Celtics in a win on November 6th.

But it was not only Michael Jordan who was playing brilliantly that season. Scottie Pippen, who averaged 18 points the year before, started looking like a true superstar himself and was arguably the second-best perimeter player in the league at that point. Pippen was regularly putting up 20 points per game and was also the league's premier triple-double threat because of his ability to rebound the ball and make plays at a rate similar to an All-Star point guard. And the team's third offensive option, Horace Grant, provided a lot of toughness inside as their leading rebounder and shot-blocker. This allowed the Bulls to win games at a rate similar to that of the dominant 80s Celtics teams that regularly won more than 60 games a year.

While it was unusual for us to not see Jordan scoring 50 or more points during the regular season, he was finally able to break the drought that year when he had 51 points and 11 rebounds against the Washington Bullets on March 19th. Five days later, he went for 50 in a win over Detroit before going for 44 against Cleveland in the very next game.

Games like those allowed Michael Jordan to average 30.1 points, 6.4 rebounds, and 6.1 assists. He was once again named the league's MVP after tallying 80 of the 96 first-place votes. Oddly enough, teammate Scottie Pippen, who had risen up to become one of the elite players in the league, actually received a first-place vote himself. Jordan and Pippen led the Chicago Bulls to an unprecedented 67-win season, their best at that point in the franchise's history.

Michael Jordan dominated the Miami Heat in the first round of the playoffs after averaging 45 points in only three games in that sweep. His best performance during that series was in Game 3 when he posted 56 points to eliminate one of the league's newest franchises. Jordan shot an amazing clip of about 61% during that dominant first-round series.

However, the Chicago Bulls would next face the toughest opponents they had during the rise of their first dynasty. The New York Knicks were primed and ready to take on whatever the Bulls were willing to give them. Plus, they had legendary head coach Pat Riley at the helm, who won four titles with the Lakers as their leader during the 1980s and was one of the best coaches in the NBA at that time.

While Pat Riley may have been known for engineering the most entertaining fast-paced team in the history of the league when he led the Showtime Lakers during the 80s, his style with the New York Knicks was different. Riley did a 180-degree turn when he switched from focusing on pushing the pace and running the floor hard to a grind-it-out physical style that slowed the pace down and punished opposing offenses in a manner similar to that of the 1980s version of the Detroit Pistons. However, Riley's Knicks had a burlier and more dominant frontline led by superstar center Patrick Ewing, former Bulls player Charles Oakley, and physical big man Anthony Mason.

The Knicks gave the Bulls a taste of their physicality early on by winning Game 1 in a shocking and surprising manner. And while Chicago did indeed lead the series when they won Games 2 and 3, New York went on to tie it all up with a win in Game 4. But, then again, Michael Jordan scored 37 points in Game 5 to put his team one win away from making a return trip to the Conference Finals. Nevertheless, the Knicks bounced back and forced Game 7 to put the defending champions' backs up against the wall.

Not willing to be brought back down to earth after ascending the heavens last season, Michael Jordan dominated the New York Knicks in Game 7. He put up 47 points, his highest in that tough series, as he went on to lead the Chicago Bulls to a 29-point win over the Knicks. It was this hard-fought series that effectively kickstarted the greatest rivalry of the 90s era.

The Eastern Conference Finals against the Cleveland Cavaliers was the renewal of the rivalry that the Bulls had with the Cavs during the end of the 80s when Jordan hit The Shot in that first-round encounter in 1989. The Cavs still retained their core, led by Mark Price, Brad Daugherty, and Larry Nance. And while they did win two games during the series, they still had no answer for Michael Jordan as he went on to average about 32 points against them to lead the Bulls to a win in six games. This win against the Cavs paved the way for the Bulls' return to the Finals to seek their second consecutive title.

During the 1992 NBA Finals, the Chicago Bulls went up against the Portland Trailblazers. The battle between the Bulls and the Blazers was hyped to be a media sensation as they tried to recreate a rivalry that was similar to Johnson versus Bird back in the 1980s. Of course, there was a reason to compare Michael Jordan to Clyde Drexler as they were arguably the two most athletic wings in the NBA at that time and they were also comparable in terms of skill set. It was Air Jordan versus the Glide in the Finals as the two superstars mirrored each other in terms of their stats, with MJ winning out in points per game while Drexler was slightly ahead in rebounds and assists. As such, Drexler went on to finish second to Jordan in the MVP votes.

Ever the competitive superstar, Michael Jordan revealed in *The Last Dance* that he did not see Clyde Drexler as someone close to his level, even though he did agree that The Glide was a threat.[xxi] Jordan proved that he truly was on an entirely different level when he had one of his most iconic moments in Game 1 of the Finals.

Throughout his career, Michael Jordan was never really a volume shooter from the three-point line and was quite judicious with his approach when shooting from that distance. Meanwhile, Clyde Drexler was described as the slightly better shooter because he was more likely to take and make a three-pointer than Jordan. That all changed in Game 1.

The Portland Trailblazers, fearing Michael Jordan's ability to get to the basket, sagged off of him throughout Game 1. MJ responded in the most Jordan-esque of ways by confidently taking whatever the Blazers were giving him. He took the three-point looks he was given and was making them. Jordan hit a total of six three-pointers in the first half alone. And when he made his sixth three-pointer, all he could do was nonchalantly shrug as if he was saying that he did not know what was happening. That gesture would later become known as "The Shrug," which players now often use when they can't seem to miss their shots.

After the "Shrug Game," Jordan ended up with 39 points. 35 of those came in the first half alone and is still a Finals record for a half. Jordan said that he was just as surprised as everyone else when his three-pointers were hitting. He even went on to say that his three-pointers started feeling like free throws in that game.[xxii] The Bulls won that outing decisively.

Even though Portland went on to tie the series after winning Games 2 and 4, the Chicago Bulls dominated Game 5 on the strength of Jordan's 46 points. Then, in Game 6, the Bulls finally put the Trailblazers away as they went on to win the NBA championship for a second straight year by winning the Finals in six games.

Michael Jordan averaged 35.8 points, 4.8 rebounds, and 6.5 assists in the Finals while thoroughly outplaying Clyde Drexler, who, in that series, did not seem like much of a rival to him. MJ won his second consecutive Finals MVP trophy and it was beginning to look like no one was equipped to take him down from the top of the mountain.

Michael Jordan had led the Bulls to back-to-back championships, similar to how Magic Johnson and Isiah Thomas did back during the 1980s. At that point in his career, he had already solidified his claim to a prominent spot in the Hall of Fame. However, winning the championship twice in a row comes with a price that not a lot of players are able to bear—the target on Jordan's back was bigger than anyone else's, given the kind of attention he was getting. For a superstar of his caliber—one that the league had never seen—MJ was under insanely intense scrutiny by both the media as well as the fans. And on top of that, the rest of the league was still out to get him.

After winning the 1992 NBA championship, Michael Jordan still had a lot of basketball to play in his schedule during the summer. He was the headliner for what became the first USA Olympic Basketball Team, which was comprised almost entirely of NBA players save for Christian Laettner, who was a collegian star for the Duke Blue Devils at the time. Going to the 1992 Olympic Games in Barcelona was not entirely troublesome for MJ but the attention he was getting in Spain from fans all over the world was overwhelming. The reception he got proved that Jordan was more than just a sensation in the states—he was a global icon and probably the most recognizable professional athlete in the entire world at the time. He was one of the biggest reasons why basketball became a global sport.

Michael Jordan went on to lead a squad dubbed "The Dream Team," which became widely regarded as the greatest basketball team ever formed. He led the team in minutes played and was second only to Charles Barkley in scoring. The Dream Team went on to win the gold medal in a spectacular fashion as they dominated every team they went up against. With that gold medal win in 1992, Michael Jordan became the first player in the history of the NBA to win the MVP Award, the NBA championship, the Finals MVP Award, and an Olympic gold medal all in one single year.

After his gold medal finish, Michael Jordan did not have much time to rest, considering that he and the Chicago Bulls still needed to prepare for a third straight title defense. As no team since the 1960s had ever won three straight championships, the Bulls were reaching for a goal that was seemingly impossible to achieve. If Jordan could achieve the impossible, it would solidify his status as one of the greatest to have ever played the game of basketball.

Early on during the 1992-93 season, Michael Jordan was a house on fire. He had multiple high-scoring games. This included a 54-point performance in an overtime loss to the Los Angeles Lakers on November 20, 1992. Then, on December 23rd, he went on to score a new season-high of 57 points in a win over the Bullets before headlining a Christmas Day victory over the New York Knicks with 42 points.

Michael Jordan then scored a new season-high of 64 points on January 16, 1993, in a loss to the Orlando Magic and their newest rookie center, Shaquille O'Neal. MJ's fourth and final 50-point game came on March 12th when he led a victory over the Charlotte Hornets with 52 big points. Overall, Jordan broke the 40-point barrier an impressive 14 times during that season to prove he was still the league's premier scorer even as youngbloods were beginning to populate the NBA.

Throughout the regular season, Michael Jordan averaged 32.6 points, 6.7 rebounds, 5.5 assists, and 2.8 steals. He led the NBA in scoring for a seventh straight year, thus tying Wilt Chamberlain's record for most scoring titles won. MJ also led the league in steals for a third straight season and was a strong consideration for the Defensive

Player of the Year Award but lost as a runner-up to Hakeem Olajuwon.

Michael Jordan, despite having gaudy numbers while leading the Chicago Bulls to 57 wins during the regular season, was unable to join the ranks of Bill Russell, Wilt Chamberlain, and Larry Bird as a winner of three straight MVP awards. Charles Barkley was named the MVP of that season after leading the Phoenix Suns to the top of the West. Jordan also proved that voter fatigue did indeed exist because he finished third behind Barkley and Olajuwon in terms of votes. But what was important for Michael Jordan was securing that third straight NBA title, even if he was not an MVP for three straight years.

The Chicago Bulls bulldozed their way through the first two rounds of the 1993 playoffs and they seemed like they were in prime shape to repeat as champions yet again. They swept their way through the Atlanta Hawks in the first round before beating the Cleveland Cavaliers in four games in the second round. Jordan's stats in those rounds mirrored the ones he had during the regular season. Meanwhile, the Bulls won five of those seven games by double digits to prove that they were still the most dominant team in the league whenever it mattered the most.

In the Eastern Conference Finals, the Chicago Bulls once again faced the New York Knicks in what seemed like the culmination of their 90s rivalry. That series against the Knicks was the most heated and most physical battle the Bulls had during their title run that season.

Patrick Ewing himself said they passionately hated each other and that the games were so tough to call because a player needed to get harmed for a referee to call a foul.[xxiii]

The Knicks during that season looked like a team that was on their way to dethroning the Bulls, just like how the Pistons dethroned the Celtics in 1988 and the Bulls dethroned the Pistons in 1991. New York won 60 games during the regular season and had homecourt advantage over the defending champions. Moreover, they also had the league's best defense led by the NBA's most physically imposing frontline and one of the premier coaches that basketball had to offer.

In the early part of the series, the Knicks looked like they were on the cusp of taking out the Bulls. They won Game 1 and then went on to defend their home court by going up 2-0 against Chicago with another win in Game 2. While the New York Knicks may have stolen the headlines with those wins against the Bulls, it was still Michael Jordan's moments before Game 2 that had the media buzzing.

Michael Jordan was always an avid gambler. He spent a lot of time gambling, to the point that the media unfairly called him addicted to it. However, Jordan always claimed that he knew when and how to stop gambling whenever he needed to. Still, the media painted a negative picture of his gambling habits, especially at a time when he did not need to gamble.

After the Bulls' practice the day before Game 2, Michael Jordan was seen leaving his hotel room in New York and was subsequently seen in Atlantic City casinos gambling. Jordan confirmed the story and he said that he went to Atlantic City with his father as a form of escape and that he was back in his room by 1:00 a.m. The pressures of being the league's top superstar and of repeating as champions that season got to him. It was his way of refocusing himself after that Game 1 loss to the New York Knicks.[xxiv]

But Jordan's innocuous trip to Atlantic City was sensationalized by the press. The media would not stop talking about it as they were criticizing MJ for going on a side trip during a time when he should have been concentrating on winning the series against the Knicks. They questioned his focus and his desire to win a third straight title that season because of how he prioritized his gambling over getting some rest and thinking of a way to get through the New York Knicks' defense.

This incidence only added fuel to the gambling-problem fire that the media was cooking up against Michael Jordan. When you are at the top, you are not only loved but you are also hated and scrutinized heavily by those who just want to see you fail. It was not only the Knicks that wanted Jordan to fall from the top—some members of the media also could not help but make it difficult for him to focus on playing and winning games with their constant barrage of negative comments.

The criticisms only grew worse when Jordan failed to perform well in Game 2 and the New York Knicks took a 2-0 lead. He did not look like himself in that game and the media once again pointed to his trip to Atlantic City as the major culprit of his failure to deliver. The aggravation was piling up to the point that not even the greatest basketball player on the planet could withstand the pressures put on him by the media.

For you to understand why that was so difficult for Jordan is for you to know that he was not a normal athlete. He was the world's biggest and most popular athlete at that time and was beginning to transcend basketball to the extent that he was a pop culture icon all over the world. Being a global superstar at that time was a remarkable accomplishment, especially when the internet and social media were yet to permeate society. In Michael Jordan's case, all eyes were constantly on *him* and not on any other basketball superstar or even any other athlete, for that matter. Getting scrutinized by the media to such a brutal degree took a heavy toll on Jordan because the ramifications were that society as a whole would start to view him as a villain and would begin to demand more out of him. It was as if the people of the sporting world thought that Michael Jordan owed them his undivided time. In short, they were not allowing him to be human. They had placed him on a pedestal that any normal human being would find impossible to live up to.

Throughout the series against the Knicks, Michael Jordan was so doggedly peppered with questions about his gambling trip that he eventually boycotted the media. You could see the look of disdain and frustration on his face, especially when he no longer needed to prove himself to the world—after all, he had just won two titles and was in a position to win a third straight championship.[xxiv] It was tiring even for a man as competitive as Michael Jordan.

While Jordan struggled in Game 3 yet again, he played the role of the facilitator and finished with 11 assists despite shooting 3 out of 18 from the field. Then, in Game 4, he tied the series up 2-2 with a classic 54-point outburst. But Game 5 was the pivotal moment of the series when MJ went for a triple-double outing of 29 points, 10 rebounds, and 14 assists. The highlight of that game came when the Knicks' 6'10" big man Charles Smith was in a position to give New York the lead with a layup at the basket but the big three of Jordan, Pippen, and Grant were all intent on denying him that basket time and time again as they all blocked his four continuous efforts at the rim.

Then, in Game 6, even though Jordan struggled with his shot, he was able to do just enough to lead the Chicago Bulls past the New York Knicks to become the first team to win a seven-game series by winning four straight games after going down 0-2 at the outset. The questions about Jordan's focus and hunger for a third straight title were squashed as he was able to vanquish his toughest opponents on his way to basketball glory that season.

That win effectively ended the rivalry between the Bulls and the Knicks while Jordan was still playing for Chicago. However, the media scrutiny of that Atlantic City trip had lingering results that eventually contributed to the most shocking news of 1993.

Media scrutiny aside, Michael Jordan and the Chicago Bulls made a third straight trip to the Finals, where they met the Phoenix Suns and their newly-crowned MVP Charles Barkley, who was arguably the second biggest superstar of the 90s because of his amazing play on the floor and his ability to gravitate media attention towards himself. And speaking of media attention, Barkley went on to say that God wanted them to win the title that season after the Suns secured their ticket to the NBA Finals.[xxv]

Unfortunately for Charles Barkley, God does not play favorites in a sport played by mortal men. But if there was someone in basketball as close to being god-like, it was Michael Jordan. MJ went on to have his best Finals at that point in his career and possibly his entire career. He averaged 41 points while scoring 40 or more points in four of the six games he played. His finest performance was on Game 4 when he had 55 points to give Chicago a 3-1 lead.

Even though Michael Jordan was primarily celebrated in that year's Finals for averaging 41 points, his best moment was actually a pass. Jordan may have been a shoot-first player but his basketball IQ was so high that he knew when to make the right plays at the right time. Case in point came in Game 6 when the Suns had a two-point lead in the final seconds of the fourth quarter and were threatening to force Game 7. Jordan received an inbound pass from Phil Jackson, who opted to make a play that initiated from the backcourt after a timeout to give Jordan a head of steam going to the basket. But instead of taking the ball all the way to the rim, MJ passed the ball right away to

Scottie Pippen the moment he realized that the defense was collapsing on him. Pippen passed the ball to Grant, who promptly gave the ball up to role player John Paxson to make a three-pointer to give the Bulls a one-point lead with a handful of seconds left. Horace Grant then proceeded to ice the series with a game-saving block as the Chicago Bulls went on to win their third straight NBA championship.

With that championship win over the Phoenix Suns, Michael Jordan set himself apart from the rest of the greats from the 70s all the way to the 90s. He led the Bulls to the NBA's first three-peat since the NBA-ABA merger. The last team to win at least three straight championships was the Boston Celtics, who won eight straight titles during the late 50s up to the middle of the 60s. But, with the NBA entirely different from what it was during Bill Russell's time back when, Michael Jordan's three-peat was arguably just as amazing as the eight straight titles the Celtics won back in the 60s. And because the Finals MVP did not yet exist back then, Jordan became the first and only player at that time to win the Finals MVP Award for three straight years. (Shaquille O'Neal would later accomplish the feat from 2000 to 2002.)

But while Michael Jordan became the world's most celebrated basketball player after that momentous achievement, the celebration for the Jordan family was as short-lived as it could possibly be because tragedy was quick to strike and take away all of MJ's happiness.

Michael Jordan's father, James Jordan Sr., was found dead in a swamp in South Carolina on August 3, 1993. It was later revealed that he was murdered on July 23rd of the same year by two teenagers who had carjacked the elder Jordan.[xxvi] The news shocked the entire world but it dealt a fatal blow to Michael Jordan's life because of how close he was with his father. Throughout his journey in the NBA, James Jordan Sr. was there to help Michael get through all the pains and hardships that accompanied the life of a basketball superstar. James Sr. was also there in all of Michael's triumphs as the latter even dedicated his first championship ring to the father who stuck with him and supported his journey to greatness since day one.

With all that said and done, the media criticisms and scrutiny were stifled a bit but there was still some baseless and hurtful speculation that attempted to connect James Jordan's death to MJ's alleged gambling problems. His father's death was the last straw to fall in what was a heavy, bittersweet year that held tragedies and issues that more than outweighed the accomplishments he had as a basketball player.

On October 6, 1993, Michael Jordan went on to shock the basketball world when he said that he was retiring from the game of basketball. The media scrutiny was too much for him to bear, but what ultimately led him to lose the will to go through another season was the death of his father. "The desire isn't there," he said in the press conference when he announced his retirement. Jordan said that he also no longer had anything else to prove.[xxvii] He had just won three straight titles and was a three-time MVP at that point in his career. The basketball world was forced to say goodbye to the sport's greatest athlete—at least for the time being.

Chapter 4: First Retirement and Brief Baseball Career

While Michael Jordan may have left the game of basketball, he did not stop being an athlete and found that he was not entirely ready to walk away from the world of sports. The greatest basketball player of all time went on to switch sports when he signed with the Chicago White Sox on February 7, 1994, to play in their minor league program. He later revealed that his desire to play baseball was a gift to his father, who had loved baseball more than basketball and was actually telling his son to try the sport after his success in the NBA.[xxviii]

Growing up, Michael Jordan had long wanted to please his father, who he once thought favored his older brother Larry because of how they bonded together more. But MJ, who had already won the NBA championship three straight times, still felt like he was yet to completely please his late father. Playing baseball was what he thought could put a smile on his father's face as he watched over Michael. As a child, the two often debated over which sporting route he should ultimately take when Michael was still a two-sport athlete. While basketball ultimately won out and gave MJ his path to greatness, baseball was once a viable consideration as he had also enjoyed and excelled at baseball while in high school and college. It was something he wanted to try so that he could leave a parting gift to his father.

After signing a contract with the White Sox and reporting to the team's spring training, he was promptly assigned to the Double-A team, the Birmingham Barons. Jordan had a good start in his career as a minor league player but he eventually went on to struggle as he only had a batting average of .202 throughout his short and brief baseball career. Jordan's struggles in baseball proved that not even the greatest athlete of one sport can easily translate his athletic gifts to another sport, especially when it came to baseball, a sport that values technique and repetition more than it does raw athletic prowess.

While Jordan was out playing baseball, the Chicago Bulls did fairly well without him. Scottie Pippen led the way for the Bulls during the 1993-94 season and went on to prove that he, too, was an MVP-caliber player after posting the best statistical averages of his career at that time. Meanwhile, teammates Horace Grant and B. J. Armstrong went on to become All-Stars that season and helped Pippen lead the Bulls to a 55-win season.

Scottie Pippen ended up finishing third in the MVP voting and had a signature play during the second round of the playoffs when he posterized Patrick Ewing in their series against the New York Knicks. That memorable dunk on Ewing is widely regarded as one of the greatest in-game dunks of all time. However, the Knicks exacted revenge on the Jordan-less Bulls by beating them in seven games. New York eventually reached the Finals where they were defeated by Hakeem Olajuwon and the Houston Rockets.

With Jordan gone, the Chicago Bulls still performed admirably and were only one win away from possibly taking the route that the Knicks took when they reached the Finals in 1994. But, as indicated by that loss to New York in the second round, it was clear that the Chicago Bulls were in dire need of their wayward alpha superstar if they wanted to return to the top of the NBA mountain.

At that time, the MLB had a lockout that carried all the way to the 1995 season. League officials were planning on starting the season with minor league players, who were not affected by the lockout. Not willing to make it to the MLB as a replacement player, Michael Jordan decided to end his brief baseball career. MLB manager Terry Francona, who managed him in Birmingham, said that Jordan had a chance to make it to the MLB for real had he spent more time batting.[xxix] But that did not transpire due to the lockout.

Meanwhile, as the Chicago Bulls struggled to replicate the comparatively successful 1993-94 season that they had had, Michael Jordan happened to be in town one fateful day in the middle of the 1994-95 season. He called friend and former teammate B. J. Armstrong and asked if they could get breakfast. Not willing to say no to the former alpha of the Bulls, Armstrong went to share a meal with Jordan. In the middle of breakfast, Armstrong invited his good friend over to go to practice with him after the meal. MJ, who had nothing else to do that day, went along with the idea of going to practice with Armstrong.[xxx]

The moment Michael Jordan joined the team's practice that day, the atmosphere completely changed and the Bulls became more competitive. When role player Jud Buechler came to practice that day and noticed that the atmosphere was different, he asked the newly acquired Ron Harper what was happening. Harper replied by simply saying that "the man's here." He was obviously referring to Michael Jordan.[xxxi]

Michael Jordan kept returning to the Bulls' practices again and again until he eventually got his desire to play basketball back. This made the media wonder whether or not he was planning on officially coming back to the game, as Jordan's appearances in the Bulls' practices became an open secret that kept people guessing. Finally, MJ confirmed everyone's suspicions by simply telling the media the words "I'm back."[xxxii]

No two words in the history of basketball had meant as much as those words coming from the game's greatest player. He was finally back after a year and a half away from the game that had made him a legend.

Chapter 5: Michael's NBA Career Part II

The Return Season

On March 19, 1995, Michael Jordan officially returned to the hardwood floor as an NBA player in a game against the Indiana Pacers wearing jersey number 45, which was his brother Larry's number and the number he used while playing baseball. Still feeling the rust of being away from competitive basketball for nearly two years, Jordan only had 19 points on a poor 7 out of 28 shooting clip in that loss to the Pacers. But while the Bulls may have lost that outing, they were happy enough that they had the franchise's greatest player back in time to help them with their playoff push.

While Jordan took his sweet time getting his groove back, he still had scoring explosions even as he was shaking off the rust. On March 28th he helped avenge the Bulls' seven-game series loss to New York the previous year by exploding for 55 points against the Knicks. Just three days before that, he had 32 in a win over the Atlanta Hawks.

Just as the Chicago Bulls had hoped, they got the push they needed when Jordan returned to the team. They won 13 of the 17 regular-season games that MJ appeared in and went on to make the playoffs with a 47-win season. In that brief 17-game campaign, Michael Jordan averaged 26.9 points, 6.9 rebounds, and 5.3 assists while shooting 41.1% from the floor. It was clear that he was yet to get back to his full basketball form, considering how low those numbers were in comparison to Jordan's pre-retirement standards.

While Jordan may have struggled in the regular season, he exploded against the Charlotte Hornets in the first round of the 1995 playoffs. In those four games, he averaged 32.3 points while shooting nearly 50% from the floor. His highlight performance was when he had 48 points in Game 1 to give the Bulls the confidence they needed to dispatch the Hornets in four games.

In the second round, however, Michael Jordan and the Bulls faced tough opponents in the form of the Orlando Magic led by the dominant powerhouse center Shaquille O'Neal and the talented all-around guard Penny Hardaway. Game 1 was an indication of what was to happen as Jordan was limited to just 19 points. It was a Nick Anderson strip on MJ that ultimately led to the Magic's win in that game. To that end, the media went on to say that Jordan did not seem like the old MJ the world knew as "No. 45 doesn't explode like No. 23 used to."[xxxiii]

Michael Jordan responded by switching back to his old No. 23 jersey even though the Bulls had retired it. He scored 38 points in Game 2 to lead the Bulls to a win. Then, in Game 3, he went for 40 points but Orlando went on to win it. The Magic eventually came out with the win in six games even though Michael Jordan averaged 31 points during that series. Orlando ultimately reached the Finals that year only to be swept by the Houston Rockets, who repeated as champions in 1995.

Losing his first playoff series since he bowed out of the 1990 playoffs in that seven-game loss to the Detroit Pistons, Michael Jordan did not look at that losing effort to the Magic as seriously as his past losses since he had just returned to the game of basketball two months ago and was still relatively out of basketball shape while adjusting to a new set of teammates. However, that loss in the 1995 playoffs was merely a blip on the radar as Jordan focused in on the upcoming 1995-96 season.

The Greatest NBA Team of All Time, Two More Titles

Michael Jordan's 1995 playoff loss might not have stung as hard as the playoff losses he had experienced in the past but it still hurt his pride due to his competitive spirit. It was what fueled him to come back stronger and better for the following season. And it all started during the summer of 1995, which turned out to be one of the most fruitful for both Jordan and the Chicago Bulls.

During the summer prior to the 1995-96 season, Michael Jordan began working on the film *Space Jam*, which is a movie about himself helping the Looney Tunes beat a group of aliens that stole the talents of several players in a basketball game. But, in the middle of filming the movie, Michael Jordan's competitive fire raged on to help prepare him for the upcoming season.

Jordan might have spent entire days in Los Angeles filming his new movie but that did not keep him away from the basketball court. It was said that he filmed from seven in the morning until seven in the evening. Most people would already be dead tired by then due to how physically taxing filming a movie can be. But Michael Jordan spent the rest of his evenings playing basketball with anyone who was in town that summer. He basically asked Warner Bros. Studio to give him a basketball court where he could work out and get back into basketball shape. And he did so by inviting NBA players over to play with him. At 32 years old, Michael Jordan still had the energy and competitive fire to train at the highest level when many other players his age were already preparing for retirement.[xxxiv]

After filming *Space Jam*, Michael Jordan spent the rest of his summer working on and refining the details of his game. The brief return during the 1994-95 season made him realize that he was no longer the same explosive athlete that could get to the basket with ease as he could when he was younger. He needed to add more weapons to an already impressive array of moves.

By looking at Jordan's shooting numbers during his first three-peat with the Chicago Bulls, you would notice how his shooting percentages gradually dropped from 1990 all the way to 1993. This was not because he was losing his touch but because he was steadily taking his game away from the basket to focus more and more on shooting jumpers. However, at that time, his style was still focused more on his ability to finish at the basket.

But, by 1995, he was 32 years old and no longer the athletic beast that he was back when he first entered the league as Air Jordan. MJ could still dunk over defenders but doing so took a lot out of him during an intensely physical 90s era. That was when he decided to make use of his post-up game, which used to be a relatively small part of his playing style in his younger days.[xxxv]

Michael Jordan refined his ability to score from the mid and the low posts by honing his footwork and the simple "bump and fade" move that became legendary during his second stint with the Chicago Bulls. The mechanics of his post game were rather simple but needed a lot of technique and repetition for any other player to do. Jordan would often act as the anchor of the triangle offense down at the mid or low post, where he could size his man up by facing up the moment he got the ball. Doing so would either make his man immediately give him space, fearing his drive, or crowd on him to take away his jump shot. This gave Jordan several options on offense as he could either drive from the post or shoot a jumper as soon as he saw enough daylight. And when he did not utilize his face-up game from the post, he often took defenders down low with a few shoulder fakes, a shimmy here and there, or a couple of dribbles before giving his man a bump to create space and go for a fading jumper.

Training from the low post while mastering the art of the midrange jumper was what ultimately allowed Michael Jordan to extend his career even though he had spent a lot of his early years getting beaten up by multiple defenders on his way to the basket. A guard playing the post was something unheard of at that time, especially during the 1990s, which is often regarded as the golden age of NBA centers.

But Michael Jordan was not the only one who improved. The Chicago Bulls, entering the 1995 training camp, looked almost entirely different from the team that won the championship three years in a row from 1991 to 1993. Save for Scottie Pippen, Jordan hardly recognized any of the other players on the roster. Horace Grant left after the 1993-94 season to join Shaq in Orlando. Meanwhile, B. J. Armstrong went to the Golden State Warriors after the 1995 Playoffs.

The new additions that Michael Jordan needed to learn how to play with were 7'2" center Luc Longley, defensive point guard Ron Harper, hot shooter Steve Kerr, and Croatian star scorer Toni Kukoč. But the biggest addition to the team was mercurial power forward Dennis Rodman, who Jordan and Pippen had had fierce battles with when he was still with the Detroit Pistons. There were questions as to whether or not Rodman would fit in with the Bulls because of how volatile his personality was and how unquestionably unpredictable he always was.

However, in terms of what he brought to the floor, Dennis Rodman was someone who no one could question. In basketball, most stars focused more on scoring points because that was what has always been the main point of playing the sport. But Rodman, an enigmatic figure, was different. He prided himself at intensely focusing on securing rebounds at the highest level possible while defending virtually any player on the court as arguably the league's most versatile defender.

Rodman always seemed to have the energy, hustle, and desire to grab rebounds over taller and bigger power forwards and centers while also pushing them around the court as their main defender. He neither had the skill nor the desire to score points but no other player in basketball was better than he was at grabbing rebounds, defending any position, and making effort plays. There might be questions about his personality but, as far as what he could do on the court, no one had a bigger heart than Dennis Rodman. That was what made him a fan favorite in Chicago.

With Dennis Rodman in the mix, the Chicago Bulls now had a new big three composed of Michael Jordan, Scottie Pippen, and the rebounding sensation. This Bulls team was different than prior Bulls rosters because all their players now had specific roles to play. Jordan was the main gun and the team's leader. Pippen played the role of a secondary option but was the team's primary on-ball defender and main playmaker. Dennis Rodman was the one who did all of the dirty work inside the paint. Ron Harper defended opposing scoring guards in place of Jordan. Toni Kukoč was the team's designated scorer off the bench. And Steve Kerr was a fallback option whom they went to for outside shooting.

In other words, this Bulls team was not composed of individual stars who could do everything but was a collection of players who knew they had specific, integral roles to play and were more than willing to focus on playing their own roles for that team. This was far different from the 1991-93 Bulls that saw Jordan and Pippen doing everything on both ends of the floor. Because everyone had a specific function on the court that they embraced by heart, the 1995-96 Chicago Bulls became the very definition of what a team should be.

By the time the season started, Michael Jordan had already adjusted to his new teammates' habits and was in the best shape of his career due to the work he put himself through during the offseason. His hard work and his dedication to his teammates showed when Chicago raced to a 23-2 start during the team's first 25 games of the 1995-96 season. In that span, Jordan averaged 30 points while breaking the 40-point barrier twice.

The Bulls eventually extended that amazing start to 41-3 and they were beginning to look like they could break the record books that season. In fact, they were virtually unbeatable and went on to go unbeaten for more than a month from December 29, 1995, to February 1, 1996. Throughout those wins, it was Jordan who fueled the way for the Bulls as the 33-year-old guard proved that he could still hang with the young guns and was still the league's best player, even after spending a year and a half away from the game.

Michael Jordan ended the season leading the league in scoring once again by averaging 30.4 points on top of 6.6 rebounds, 4.3 assists, and 2.2 steals. He secured his eighth scoring title and went on to break the league record he had previously shared with Wilt Chamberlain. Jordan was such a phenomenal scorer that season in a slow-paced era that the guard who came closest to his scoring average was Mitch Richmond, who averaged 23.1 points. All the other high-scoring players that season were centers and power forwards, given that the 90s was a decade dominated by big men. But, even so, Hakeem Olajuwon's 26.9 points per game were a distant second behind Jordan's scoring average that season.

As impressive an accomplishment as it was for Michael Jordan to win his eighth scoring title at the advanced age of 33, becoming the oldest leading scorer in NBA history (a record previously held by Jerry West, who won the scoring championship at 31 years old in 1970), what was even more impressive was the fact that he led the Chicago Bulls to the league's first 70-win season. They ended the regular season with 72 wins and only 10 losses to break the 69-win record previously held by Jerry West's Lakers back in the 1971-72 season.

By accomplishing a personal feat that coincided with the biggest team accomplishment in the NBA's regular season, Michael Jordan was voted as the league's MVP for the fourth time in his career. He almost became the first unanimous winner of the award when he garnered all but five first-place votes. Nevertheless, the newly crowned four-time MVP playing for the league's best regular-season team still had one ultimate goal in mind—to win a championship. After all, 72-10 would not mean a thing without a ring.

The road to a fourth ring kicked off with a dominant first-round trouncing of the Miami Heat. An old nemesis was back—Pat Riley, who had given the Bulls a lot of trouble when he was still with the Knicks, was coaching the Heat. But Miami never stood a chance and were swept out of the first round on a losing margin of 23 points per game.

Next, Jordan and the Bulls made short work of an entirely different New York Knicks team. MJ averaged 36 points in five games. Then, in the Eastern Conference Finals, the Chicago Bulls avenged their loss from a year ago by sweeping the Orlando Magic in four games. While the matchup between the 7'1", 300-pound powerhouse center Shaquille O'Neal and the 6'7" lean-and-mean Dennis Rodman was the highlight of the series, Jordan finished the Magic off with a majestic 45-point performance in Game 4.

The win over the Magic secured the Bulls' return trip to the Finals, which they last made in 1993 when Jordan was in the final year of his first stint with the Chicago Bulls. They went on to face the Seattle SuperSonics, a high-scoring, 64-win team led by All-Star point guard

Gary Payton and athletic star big man Shawn Kemp, who seemed to be good enough to pose a challenge to the streaking Chicago Bulls.

However, the Bulls rampaged through the Sonics in the first three games of the Finals. They went on to win Games 1 and 3 by double digits and managed to pull off a 3-0 lead over the Sonics. At that point, and since no team in NBA history had ever come back from a 0-3 deficit in a seven-game series, Michael Jordan seemed to be in prime position to win his fourth NBA championship ring.

Michael Jordan, in the first three games of the series, averaged 31 points. However, it bears mentioning that the new Defensive Player of the Year, Gary Payton, who was the first and only point guard to ever win that award, was not guarding Jordan in those first three games due to a calf injury. Payton returned and took on that responsibility after Game 3, defending MJ with his trademark physical play.

The switch worked, as the Bulls ended up losing Games 4 and 5 with Gary Payton guarding Jordan. Payton, in *The Last Dance*, gave himself credit by saying that he tired Jordan out with his physical brand of defense. But when Jordan saw the video clip of Payton saying those words, he brushed it off and said that he had no problem with the man called The Glove.

Nevertheless, the stats showed that Gary Payton did most definitely limit Michael Jordan in Games 4 and 5 after the latter went for only 24.5 points on a poor 41.5 shooting clip. The trouble carried on into Game 6, where Jordan shot 5 out of 19 from the field to go for only

111

22 points. Statistically speaking, The Glove did indeed put the clamps on the greatest player in the world, who shot 36.7% from the floor and scored 23.7 points from Game 4 to 6.

But even the brilliant defensive play of Gary Payton was enough. The Chicago Bulls that season were the greatest team in the history of the NBA for a good reason. Jordan may have been their top option on offense, but the Bulls were more than the sum of their parts and their arsenal ran deep. After losing Games 4 and 5, Chicago denied the Seattle SuperSonics and went on to win Game 6 to secure the franchise's fourth NBA title.

Winning his first NBA championship since his father died in 1993, the four-time champion and four-time Finals MVP Michael Jordan was seen weeping on the floor of the locker room clutching the ball in his arms. It was Father's Day when the Bulls won the 1996 NBA championship and Jordan, who averaged his worst Finals numbers of 27.3 points on 41.5% shooting from the floor, could not help but think of his father when he reached the basketball apex once again.

This was a far cry from the celebratory Michael Jordan back in 1992 and in 1993. It was an emotional moment for a player who dedicated another momentous achievement to the man who was always there to help him achieve his goals. Again, the world saw how human Michael Jordan could be as he cried and wept like any other normal person would in that situation.

Yet, no matter how human he might be from an emotional perspective, he was still a super-human presence on the court. Jordan had secured his fourth NBA title in a season that was one of the best the world had ever witnessed.

The 2015-16 Golden State Warriors would later break the Bulls' 72-10 record but they failed to win the title that season. As such, the 1995-96 Chicago Bulls remain as the greatest team in league history. Of course, they were led by the man widely regarded as the greatest basketball player of all time.

Following that 72-win season, people were expecting the Chicago Bulls to lose their hunger and desire to win more games and championships and simply cruise along the regular season before going off in the playoffs. But that would never happen as long as you have Michael Jordan as a teammate. Competing hard came first for the greatest of all time.

Impressively, the Chicago Bulls dominated the regular season once again on their way to a 49-6 start through their first 55 games. Along the way, the 33-year-old Michael Jordan had memorable moments as a scorer. He had 50 in their fourth game of the season. Then, on January 21, 1997, he finished a win over the New York Knicks with 51 big points while uncharacteristically hitting five three-pointers in that game.

At such a rate, the Chicago Bulls seemed to be on pace to equal or even beat the season they had a year ago, especially with Michael

Jordan and Scottie Pippen playing like the superstars they were. However, the Bulls stumbled a bit in the latter part of the season when they lost Dennis Rodman, who only played 55 games that year due to an injury. Chicago could have won 72 games again but they lost three of their final four games to end the regular season. But 69 wins still placed them at second all-time in terms of their regular-season record back then.

Michael Jordan averaged 29.6 points, 5.9 rebounds, and 4.3 assists during the regular season. He once again led the league in scoring and won the scoring title as a then 34-year old player a total of nine times at that point in his career. Before Jordan won the scoring title last season when he was 33, the oldest player to lead the league in scoring was Jerry West at 31.

No other player in the history of the game had ever led the NBA in scoring past the age of 30 partly due to how most 30-year old or above star players are more inclined to preserve themselves for the playoffs, or due to the fact that most players at that age are already willing to cede the scoring title to younger players who are still trying to make a name for themselves. But Jordan did so at the age of 34 at a time when the league had a lot of other great superstars that could score points in bunches and in an efficient manner. Names such as Karl Malone, David Robinson, and Shaquille O'Neal were only a few of such players.

But how did Michael Jordan do it at his age while shooting an efficient 48.6% shooting clip as a shooting guard? Well, the answer is his efficiency and mastery of the midrange jump shot. Shot data during the 1996-97 season shows that nearly 60% of Michael Jordan's shot attempts were two-point jumpers beyond 10 feet. And, amazingly, he was making nearly 50% of those shots while shooting better from beyond 16 feet than he did from 10 to 16 feet. This goes to show that Jordan had mastered the art of making long jump shots over the outstretched arms of his defenders.

Michael Jordan's efficiency as a shot-creator from the midrange area during the 1996-97 season was a far cry from the type of player he was several years ago when he was an athletic demon who preferred to score his points near the basket. During that season, he was only 57th overall in points in the paint and was 54th in the league in terms of three-pointers made.[xxxvi] What those numbers tell you is that the majority of Jordan's points came largely from the two-point field goals he was making from the midrange area.

Out of all the players who attempted 300 midrange shots that season, Jordan led the league with 547 conversions. Glenn Robinson was a far second with 391 midrange conversions. Similarly, Michael Jordan ranked third in efficiency in midrange makes as he converted 49.5% of them despite attempting over a thousand midrange shots the entire season. His midrange makes were even a lot more than the total number of attempts that hot shooter Reggie Miller, regarded as the best shooter of the 1990s, had from the midrange area that season.[xxxvi]

So, what does Jordan's efficiency from the midrange area during the 1996-97 season mean? It simply shows how high of a skill level he had back when he was a 34-year old shooting guard playing for the league's best team. Nowadays, the long midrange shot is by far the most inefficient shot a player can make because of the degree of difficulty that is usually involved in a shot that has low rewards. But Jordan was taking thousands of these shots and was making half of them.

And when Michael Jordan was playing with the Bulls that season, it was not as if he was taking easy midrange shots that came from plays designed to open him up. Back then, the floor spacing was not as good as it is during the modern era of the NBA. Moreover, Jordan was the only true scoring threat that the Bulls had. That meant that things were a lot more difficult for him considering that he did not have a lot of space to work with when looking for his shot and that defenses were more than likely designed to prevent him from getting a good look.

In other words, MJ had to create most of his shots on his own without relying on a system that designed open looks for him or on other players to absorb defensive attention away from him. His midrange shooting was a product of a steady diet of his patented one-dribble pull-up jumper over outstretched arms and his trademark turnaround fadeaway jump shot from the high post. It takes an insanely high degree of technique and repetition to be able to hit those types of jumpers at an era when defenses were much more physical and when

116

floor spacing was still weak. Nevertheless, Jordan proved himself a cut above the rest when he was leading the league in scoring while hitting the midrange shot, the most inefficient shot in the NBA, at an efficient clip. His 1996-97 season is proof that there is no reason for players to shy away from taking midrange jumpers as long as they can hit them at an incredibly efficient rate.

Steve Smith, one of the most talented defenders of the late 1990s, described what it was like defending Michael Jordan. Unlike defending Reggie Miller, whose style was to run around the floor without the ball hoping he lost his defender in a pick, Jordan took pleasure in beating you with the ball in his hands. The moment he caught the ball and sized his defender up, he would keep his man guessing what would happen next to the point that all a defender could do was try his best to contest a shot and hope it would miss. Smith said that Jordan's moves had no pattern that a defender could dissect because of how wide MJ's one-on-one arsenal was. And when he shot his signature fadeaway, it was basically game over for any defender whose only hope was that Michael Jordan was off his game.[xxxvi]

However, in what was one of the closest two-man races for the MVP Award, Michael Jordan failed to win a fifth MVP when Utah's Karl Malone won it for the first time in his career after leading the Utah Jazz to the franchise's best season. Malone received 63 out of 115 first-place votes while Jordan received the other 52. Michael Jordan would use this MVP loss to Malone as a means of motivating himself later on during the playoffs when they inevitably met in the Finals.

Similar to last season, the 1996-97 Chicago Bulls cruised their way through the Eastern Conference and only lost two games on their way to the Finals, wherein they went on to face Karl Malone and the Utah Jazz. Up to that point, Jordan was averaging over 30 points per game in the 13 games he played during the postseason before getting to the Finals.

The Utah Jazz were an interesting team that was seemingly at the precipice of NBA greatness after failing to make it to the Finals time and time again since the 1980s, even though they had two superstars in Karl Malone and John Stockton. Together, Malone and Stockton formed arguably the greatest pick-and-roll tandem the league had ever seen. But it was only during the 1996-97 season that things clicked for them, despite their relatively advanced age.

Game 1 of the Finals was an interesting bout as neither team was willing to give the other an edge. The Bulls and the Jazz traded blows in what almost felt like a boxing match. Tied 82 all with 7.5 seconds left on the clock, the Bulls had possession of the ball and called timeout. The play was simple—give Jordan the ball. Michael Jordan received the inbound pass beyond the left wing before isolating himself with the Jazz's best perimeter defender, Bryon Russell. Jordan sized Russell up and was dribbling towards his right before he took a quick dribble to the left, creating just enough room to hit a jumper at the buzzer to win the game for the Chicago Bulls. Just another day at the office for Michael Jordan.

Michael Jordan led the Chicago Bulls in Game 2 after posting 31 points in his dramatic Game 1 performance. The Bulls won the second game of the Finals convincingly as Jordan finished with 38 points, 13 rebounds, and 9 assists. While Chicago may have raced to a 2-0 lead, the Utah Jazz found inspiration at home in what was a 2-3-2 Finals format back then. Utah won Games 3 and 4 and were threatening to take the lead in Game 5 before one of the most iconic games in NBA history transpired right before the entire world's very eyes.

In *The Last Dance*, Michael Jordan's crew narrated what had happened the night before Game 5 in Utah. They said that MJ suddenly felt hungry in the middle of the night. However, room service was not available and the only place open was a local pizza place. With no choice, they ordered pizza for Michael Jordan, who ate the entire thing all by himself.[xxxvii] But, after eating the pizza, Michael Jordan suddenly felt ill and he was vomiting like crazy the remainder of the night while complaining of stomach aches, according to his personal trainer Tim Grover. The team doctor said that it was food poisoning.

The symptoms carried over to the next day when Jordan spent the entire moments before the game vomiting. Needless to say, he was not feeling entirely well as the media described him as having "flu-like symptoms" entering Game 5.

Michael Jordan eventually found the strength to get up from his hotel room bed before six in the evening and made it in time to the arena before tip-off at around seven in the evening. He obviously did not look like himself as he struggled to even walk. But the Bulls needed their leader for that pivotal game. A sick Jordan was still better than 90% of what the league had to offer at that time. He still had the mental will to suit up and play for the Chicago Bulls, who were counting on him in the pivotal moment of the Finals.

Early on during the game, Jordan struggled, still looking ill as he was missing his shots and allowed the Utah Jazz to take a swift 16-point lead. But MJ suddenly started making his shots while focusing all of his efforts on the offensive end. He scored 17 points in the second quarter alone to give the Chicago Bulls the hope they needed to win that game. Then again, Jordan suddenly found himself fatigued during the third quarter—he was visibly unable to even sit upright when he was on the bench.

Somehow finding the strength and will to push through, Michael Jordan played the entire fourth quarter and scored 15 points in the final 12 minutes of the game. It was his three-pointer with 25 seconds left on the clock that gave the Chicago Bulls the cushion they needed to win the game. And when John Stockton missed a free throw that would have helped the Utah Jazz get within striking distance, a relieved Jordan collapsed into Scottie Pippen's arms after giving everything that he had to win that game.

Scoring 38 points while playing 44 minutes the entire game, Michael Jordan had just given the world one of the most memorable performances in NBA Finals history. His performance would be dubbed as "The Flu Game" due to how he was able to perform at such a high level despite showing flu-like symptoms that sapped his strength to the point that he had trouble standing up at times during that game.

Jordan's Flu Game is the very embodiment of mind over matter. So long as you have a goal in mind and you are willing to do whatever it takes to achieve it, you will be able to push through against all of the odds stacked against you.

Game 6 showed another memorable moment that the world knows too well because of how Michael Jordan was willing to defer to his teammates whenever he needed to do so. The Bulls were down by nine early in the fourth quarter but somehow managed to take the lead with a 10-0 run. From then on, they traded baskets with the Utah Jazz until they were left tied at 86 apiece with seconds left on the clock.

The Chicago Bulls called a timeout and drew a play. Role player Steve Kerr, who is known for being the most accurate jump shooter on that Bulls team, was visibly telling Jordan that he would be ready to take the shot if MJ was going to pass him the ball. When the play started, the Jazz doubled Jordan as soon as he got the ball because they were not going to let him beat them again the same way he did in Game 1. But Michael Jordan immediately found Steve Kerr as soon as John Stockton left his defensive assignment. Proving his worth, Kerr hit a 17-foot shot that gave the Bulls the lead with five seconds left on the clock. In the ensuing Jazz play, Scottie Pippen deflected an inbound pass that could have given Utah a chance at tying or winning the game.

The overall team effort that the Chicago Bulls displayed in those final seconds showcased how willing they were to rely on one another to win the game. That said, it was Jordan's willingness to trust his teammates that ultimately allowed him to secure his fifth NBA championship and fifth Finals MVP trophy after averaging 32.3 points in what was his most memorable Finals series at that point in his career.

But the question at that point was whether or not the Chicago Bulls were still willing to do it all again after they had already secured five championships under the Michael Jordan era. There were uncertainties looming even as they had just secured their place at the top of the mountain yet again. All of those questions were answered in what eventually became MJ's last season with the Chicago Bulls.

The Last Dance

Things became uncertain for the Chicago Bulls during the 1997 offseason. The team's general manager, Jerry Krause, became public enemy number one due to a number of reasons. Aside from angering both Michael Jordan and Scottie Pippen several years ago when he had called Toni Kukoč "the future" of the team, he also fractured his relationship with Phil Jackson by making it public that he was aiming to replace the five-time champion coach by the end of the 1997-98 season.

Meanwhile, Scottie Pippen, who was locked into a long-term deal that did not seem lucrative enough for a player of his caliber, felt like Krause was not treating him well in the financial sense. This forced Pippen into strong-arming the front office to trade him while he was recovering from an off-season surgery he purposely delayed to try to cut a lucrative deal with Jerry Krause.[xxxviii] As such, he was unavailable during much of the early part of the 1997-98 season.

Michael Jordan, who was shocked at the news that Jackson was going to get replaced at the end of the upcoming season, publicly stated that he was not going to play for another head coach and that he would rather retire than to play for anyone other than Phil. Thus, it became public knowledge that the greatest player of all time was going to retire by the end of the 1997-98 season.

Phil Jackson, amidst all the uncertainties and issues surrounding the team, used this to his advantage and made it into the team's rallying cry. He began calling the final season as "the last dance," which ultimately became the main topic of the 10-part docu-series of the same title. It was going to be MJ's and Phil's final stint with the Bulls. Meanwhile, no one was even certain as to Pippen's status with the team due to the trade rumors surrounding his name while he was recovering from an injury.

In the early portion of the 1997-98 season, the Chicago Bulls looked mortal compared to their unbeatable version of the last two seasons. They went 12-9 during the first 21 games of the season, primarily because Michael Jordan had to shoulder the burden all by himself without Scottie Pippen in the mix. That was when the Bulls realized how important Pippen truly was for them since it was becoming clear that a 35-year old Jordan was not going to be able to do it all by himself at that point in his career.

It took Jordan asking more from Dennis Rodman, Toni Kukoč, Luc Longley, and Ron Harper to steer the ship back in the right direction. The Chicago Bulls managed to improve as the season went by and only added four more losses by the end of January 1998, primarily because they had already gotten Scottie Pippen back when the new year started.

Michael Jordan was the Chicago Bulls' lone representative in the annual All-Star Game, which featured several of the league's brightest young stars at a time when the NBA was seeing an influx of talented players that grew up watching MJ. One such player was Kobe Bryant, who got drafted into the NBA in 1996 as a 17-year old high school phenom and went on to become the youngest All-Star in 1997 at the age of 19. Bryant was selected as an All-Star starter primarily because he was already showing flashes of star power akin to what it might take to become the next Jordan.

In the locker room prior to the All-Star Game, Michael Jordan was seen talking to his fellow All-Stars, saying "that little Laker boy's going to take everybody one-on-one" after spending the season watching Bryant trying to take the entire league on by himself, much the same way MJ did back when he was a rookie. Jordan went on to say that he was going to make things one-on-one between him and Bryant if Kobe wanted it to happen in the game.[xxxix]

True enough, Jordan and Kobe had their moments of one-on-one in that game but it seemed like the NBA's greatest player had the advantage over the young gun. Nevertheless, Bryant had his own moments and went on to lead the Western All-Stars in scoring. But it was Michael Jordan who ended up winning the game and the All-Star MVP trophy. Still, that moment seemed like a passing of the torch from the 35-year old Michael Jordan to the 19-year old Kobe Bryant.

When Scottie Pippen returned from his injury, another problem arose. Dennis Rodman, who Michael Jordan had asked to be a "model citizen" all season long while they were waiting for Pippen to recover because they did not have any time to waste on his shenanigans, felt like being someone he was not made him crazy. He suddenly felt the urge to reward himself in the middle of the season and asked Phil Jackson if he could go to Las Vegas for a 48-hour period for a short vacation.

Michael Jordan was against the idea of Rodman taking a leave of absence from the team to go to Vegas, thinking that they were never going to see him again if he was allowed to let loose. But Phil Jackson realized that Dennis Rodman had to be himself if the Bulls wanted their last dance to be a successful one. Rodman was allowed to go to Las Vegas.

Unsurprisingly, Dennis Rodman did not return on time as the 48-hour trip turned out to be longer. He did return to Chicago but he still thought that he needed some time off for himself. It took Michael Jordan himself to go to Rodman's apartment right across the street from the Bulls' arena to drag him out of his bed and to force him to practice. To Rodman's credit, he outshined everyone else on the team when Phil Jackson forced them to do a conditioning drill that would allow the mercurial superstar to get back into basketball shape after his short vacation in Vegas. From then on, Dennis Rodman returned to his old self and became part of the reason why the Bulls' second half of the season was successful.[xl]

In the Chicago Bulls' final 36 games, they ended up losing only seven of them, largely because of how they were able to get the gang back together fully healthy and mentally prepared to make the last dance a memorable one. This allowed the Chicago Bulls to win 62 games during the regular season to tie the Utah Jazz for the league's best record.

Michael Jordan, in his last regular season with the Chicago Bulls, led the league for a tenth and final time in scoring by averaging 28.7 points on a shooting clip of 46.5%. Due to the fact that he needed to carry the scoring load more during the early portion of the regular season, Jordan had a total of 12 40-point games, even at the advanced age of 35 years old. His best scoring performance was when he had 49 points against the Los Angeles Clippers during the early portion of the season.

For his efforts in leading the Chicago Bulls to the best record in the league when Pippen was not around, and due to how the world was expecting him to leave by the end of the season, Michael Jordan won his fifth and final MVP award. By winning five MVP trophies, Jordan was tied with the great Bill Russell at second all-time in most MVPs won. They both trailed Kareem Abdul-Jabbar, who won the MVP six times.

Unlike the last two seasons, the Chicago Bulls faced diversity this time around. They still managed to beat the first two rounds, losing only one game in the process while quickly dispatching the New Jersey Nets and the Charlotte Hornets in the process of making the Eastern Conference Finals yet again. However, they faced a roadblock in the form of the Indiana Pacers.

At that time, the Indiana Pacers sported a group of players that played the game in a gritty and physical way. Led by hot shooter Reggie Miller, the Pacers had a collection of players that were willing to grind it out and make it difficult for their opponents to come out of games in one piece. Of course, it also helped that Larry Bird, one of the greatest players of all time, coached the team.

The Chicago Bulls may have won the first two games at home but those wins were precarious at best because the Bulls only won them both by six points. Jordan was stellar in those outings after averaging 36 points in Games 1 and 2. However, the results showed that the Pacers were there to make things difficult for the Chicago Bulls.

In Game 3, the Indiana Pacers went on to win by 2 points even as Michael Jordan scored 30 points. The formula was clear. Indiana may not have had a way of stopping Jordan but they were more than capable of stopping the rest of the Bulls' roster while also making the Chicago defense work hard. This paved the way for Game 4, where Reggie Miller had his most iconic moment.

The Bulls and the Pacers once again played a grind-it-out style in Game 4 as they traded blow after blow until it all came down to the last play of the game to decide who would win it. Chicago was up by one point with a few ticks left on the clock. The Pacers had possession of the ball and drew up a play designed for Reggie Miller, their best player. Before the ball was inbounded into play, Miller was moving all over the floor, gave Jordan a slight nudge at the top of the key to free himself up, and raced all the way to the right wing to shoot and make an open three-pointer that won the game for the Pacers. Miller, in 2020, admitted that he did indeed push Jordan in a play that may have looked like an offensive foul.[xli] Nevertheless, the series was tied and it looked like the two-time defending champs had their backs up against the wall.

In Game 5, the Chicago Bulls won a pivotal bout, which turned out to be the only lopsided game of the entire series. Jordan had 29 points in that game before going into Game 6 with 35 points. However, the Indiana Pacers were able to force a seventh and deciding game with a win in Game 6. This was the first time Michael Jordan played a Game 7 in the Eastern Conference Finals since winning the 1992 Eastern Conference Finals against the Knicks.

While the Indiana Pacers may have had the momentum on their side coming into Game 7, they ended up falling short as the Chicago Bulls found the strength to hang on to the lead in that game to win the series on their home floor. Jordan, who had 28 in Game 7, averaged 31.7 points in the Eastern Conference Finals on his way to his sixth and final appearance in the NBA Finals. This win against the Pacers set up a rematch against the well-rested Utah Jazz, who swept the Western Conference Finals and had 10 days of rest while waiting for their opponents from the East.

True enough, the well-rested Jazz pounced on a tired Bulls team that only had two days of rest coming into the Finals. Michael Jordan did not look tired when he had 35 points in Game 1. But, then again, the Utah Jazz had more energy that night and managed to draw first blood by three points when Scottie Pippen missed a three-pointer at the buzzer. At that point, it seemed as if both Karl Malone and John Stockton were on their way to winning a well-deserved first NBA championship.

The Chicago Bulls were able to tie the series up and steal home court away from their tough opponents when they went on to put together a fourth-quarter rally that allowed them to escape Game 2 with a win. This was their first win against the Jazz all season long, as they had not won a single game against the Utah Jazz during the regular season.

When the series shifted over to Chicago for Games 3 to 5, the Bulls protected home court well enough in the first two games at home. In Game 3, the Chicago Bulls' defense was at its best when they managed to limit the Utah Jazz to the lowest points scored in the history of the NBA Finals. MJ only needed to play 32 minutes in that game as the Bulls limited the Jazz to only 54 points. In Game 4, the Bulls raced to a 3-1 lead when they held on to a four-point win with Jordan scoring 34 points. The Jazz, not willing to go down so easily, won Game 5 to shift the series back in Utah, where they had homecourt advantage.

Game 6 of the 1998 NBA Finals was Michael Jordan's finest moment as a professional basketball player. Scottie Pippen, who already had a back injury coming into the series, aggravated it after scoring a dunk in the opening basket of the game.[xlii] This injury set up what was going to be a dramatic Game 6 for both Jordan and the entire Chicago

Bulls team as Scottie Pippen had to spend time in and out of the locker room to get his injury treated by their medical squad.

Michael Jordan held the fort down while an injured Scottie Pippen spent a considerable amount of time off the court for most of the game in an attempt to preserve him until they needed his services in the final stretch of that all-important bout. At that moment, the Bulls' coaching staff had decided that Pippen would just be on the court to serve as a decoy and a defender rather than to force him to perform at a stellar level.

At the end of the third quarter, the Utah Jazz had a five-point lead. But they let the Chicago Bulls run in the fourth quarter as MJ and the rest of his boys went on to tie the game up at 83 with under a minute left in the game. John Stockton quelled the Bulls' run by going for a three-pointer that gave the Jazz a three-point lead with 42 seconds left on the clock. This play was what allowed Jordan to take over the game and have the three most important plays of his entire career.

Michael Jordan scored a layup that allowed the Chicago Bulls to get within a single point with under 19 seconds left on the clock. However, the Utah Jazz had the ball in what was supposed to be the final play of the game, considering that they only needed to secure the ball and force Chicago to play the foul game.

Knowing that the ball was going to go to Karl Malone down in the low post, Michael Jordan prepared himself for what was going to be the most important defensive play of his entire career. Malone did indeed catch the ball down low while backing off Dennis Rodman. However, what The Mailman did not know was that Jordan gambled and left his defensive assignment to sneak from the baseline and strip the ball away from Karl Malone with 16 seconds left on the clock.

But, instead of taking a timeout, Michael Jordan dribbled the ball up the court all on his own without passing the ball to any other player. He stopped about six feet away from the right wing three-point line, looking up at the clock all while his defender, Bryon Russell, was waiting on what he was about to do. At that moment, the entire world realized that Jordan was not going to pass the ball—he was going to win it all on his own.

Michael Jordan allowed the clock to get milked down to under 10 seconds before making a move. He dribbled to his right while Russell was hounding him. With about nine seconds left, he made a quick dribble to the top of the circle, stopped on a dime while Russell was falling down thinking that MJ was going to take the ball all the way to the basket. While some people thought that Jordan may have pushed his defender off to get him off-balance, there was no foul called as it was evident to the officials that it was Russell's momentum that took him off-balance.

With no defender in sight, Michael Jordan gathered the ball, went to his shooting motion, and drilled the most memorable jump shot of his entire career to score his 45th point of the game and to give the Chicago Bulls the lead with about five seconds left on the clock. Over at the other end, the Utah Jazz tried to make a play after calling a timeout but they were unable to execute it. The Chicago Bulls went on to win the game and to secure their sixth championship under Michael Jordan.

Winning his sixth and final NBA championship and Finals MVP, Michael Jordan's game-winning shot to secure the series remains his most iconic moment. His final three plays—the layup, the steal, and the shot—were what the Bulls needed at a time when they were missing their second offensive option. And they were the final gifts that Michael Jordan gave to Chicago as those three plays were going to be the final ones he would have as a Bulls player.

Michael Jordan had played his final game for the Chicago Bulls and had drilled his final jumper for the franchise that drafted him back in 1984.

Second Retirement

As the Chicago Bulls celebrated the franchise's sixth title, fans began clamoring for Michael Jordan to return for one more season. From the looks of it, he was more than capable of going through the grind of another regular season. At 35 years old, he had just led the NBA in scoring and went on to perform at his best throughout the playoffs until he won the 1998 NBA title.

However, it was becoming inevitable that he would not be returning to the court. Phil Jackson's contract had just expired and the Bulls' front office did not have any plans of bringing him back. Meanwhile, both Scottie Pippen and Dennis Rodman were also planning on leaving the team. This all happened in the middle of a lockout that made everything unclear.

By the end of the lockout, Jordan announced on January 13, 1999, that he would be leaving the game of basketball to retire. He had long wanted to retire from the NBA on his own terms. Back in the middle of the 1997-98 season, he revealed to media personality Ahmad Rashad that he wanted to leave basketball at the top of his game instead of waiting for the time that he could no longer play the sport at the highest level. That was what happens to most NBA players; they play and play until their body tells them they could no longer do it.[xliii]

But Michael Jordan, again, wanted to leave on his own terms—in peak form, and not under the emotional duress that had influenced his earlier, brief retirement following the tragic death of his father. He did so by retiring from the NBA as the game's best player after leading the league in scoring, winning the All-Star MVP, earning the MVP Award, and leading the Bulls to their sixth title under his leadership all while garnering the Finals MVP nod in the process.

Michael Jordan retired from the game of basketball as a 12-time All-Star, a 10-time scoring champion, a 10-time All-NBA First Team member, a Defensive Player of the Year, a five-time Most Valuable Player, a six-time NBA champion, a six-time NBA Finals MVP, and as the NBA's all-time points per game leader with an average of 31.5 points. At that point in time, there was no doubt that he was already the greatest player to have ever set foot in the NBA, and he retired knowing that he was still the best.

After Michael Jordan retired, the Chicago Bulls organization imploded and could not seem to achieve the same kind of success again. Phil Jackson moved to Los Angeles to coach the Lakers, who he led to three straight titles from 2000 to 2002 while coaching the dominant Shaquille O'Neal and Jordan's heir apparent, Kobe Bryant.

Scottie Pippen moved to Houston to join forces with fellow veterans Hakeem Olajuwon and Charles Barkley before moving to Portland, where he was able to make it to the conference finals in 2000. Pippen retired as a Bull during the 2003-04 season. Meanwhile, Dennis Rodman struggled to find his place in the league and finally retired after playing only 35 games since winning the 1998 NBA Finals.

Had the Bulls not decided to break the team apart by keeping Phil Jackson, Michael Jordan might have decided to stay for at least one more season during the 1999 campaign and there could have been a possibility that he would have won a seventh title, especially if they were able to find a way to keep Pippen and Rodman. After all, the 1999 season was shortened due to the lockdown. The elder Bulls would have been well-rested and could have more than likely made the Finals, especially considering that it was an old and battered New York Knicks that represented the East during the 1999 NBA Finals.

Nevertheless, things happened for a reason and Michael Jordan had to leave the game on his own terms.

Michael Jordan returned to the NBA during January of 2000 as the Washington Wizards' new president of basketball operations. During his time running the Wizards, he was most notable for his unpopular decision as an executive as he went on to use the 2001 top overall pick to draft Kwame Brown straight out of high school (an NBA first). Unfortunately, Brown never really lived up to expectations.

Chapter 6: Michael's NBA Career Part III

Two years from the day he announced his second retirement from the game of basketball, Michael Jordan expressed in 2001 his desire to come back to the NBA to once again play the sport. This time, however, he was going to do it as the Washington Wizard's president of basketball operations. He said that his decision to return to the game was inspired by how his good friend Mario Lemieux returned to the NFL after his retirement.[xliv]

Prior to making his return official, there was already speculation that Michael Jordan was planning on returning to the sport. He had spent the entire summer of 2001 training and working on his conditioning while inviting NBA players over to play and train with him. Jordan dismissed that by saying that he was simply trying to lose some weight. However, when he hired his former Chicago Bulls head coach Doug Collins to take over the job as head coach of the Washington Wizards, it was becoming obvious that he indeed was coming back.[xlv]

At 38 years old and turning 39 that season, Michael Jordan returned to a league that had become vastly different from when he played his final game as a Bull in 1998. Three years had passed and a new crop of superstars had taken over the league. The best player at that time was the hulking center named Shaquille O'Neal, who was responsible for eliminating Jordan from the playoffs back in 1995. The other great players of that time were big men Tim Duncan and Kevin Garnett.

Meanwhile, the shooting guard position had also evolved thanks in large part to how Michael Jordan inspired an entire generation of younger shooting guards. High-flying sensation Vince Carter, a product of North Carolina as well, was widely regarded as an athlete similar in build and prowess to a young Michael Jordan. Tracy McGrady, regarded as the greatest high school player ever, was also showing signs of his Jordan-esque talents by putting up 25 to 30 points a night. While he may have been small, the six-footer Allen Iverson, who was famous for crossing Jordan over as a rookie, became the league's premier backcourt scorer and had scoring confidence similar to MJ's but with a swagger all his own.

However, it was Kobe Bryant, who had already won the title twice at that point in his career, who was the closest to Michael Jordan in terms of his overall abilities at the shooting guard position. Since his younger years during the late 1990s, Kobe began asking Michael for pointers and tips on how to become a great player. Bryant patterned his game after Jordan's style and eventually went on to become one of the greatest shooting guards in the history of the NBA. The two remained close since Bryant's early years in the league up until his untimely death in January of 2020.

Meanwhile, back in 2001, there were not a lot of things that Michael Jordan could do at the age of 38 and he was not expected to lead a team to a championship, considering that the Wizards lacked a depth of talent outside of shooting guard Rip Hamilton, who credits his amazing midrange game to MJ's teachings. For the first time in his career, a slower yet bigger Jordan moved over to the small forward spot that season.

The elderly Jordan did not have a lot of great moments at that point in his career but he did still manage to score 44 points on November 16, 2001, against no less than his old rivals, the Utah Jazz. Then, on December 29th, he went on to become the oldest player to score at least 50 points in a single game when he had 51 points in a win over the Charlotte Hornets. It would take nearly two decades for another player to break this record.

Then, in wins against the Cleveland Cavaliers and the Phoenix Suns late in January of 2002, Michael Jordan poured in back-to-back 40-point games by going for 40 and 41 respectively. However, later in the season, he had to cut his year short after suffering torn cartilage in his right knee. Age had finally caught up with the man regarded as the greatest of all time.

Michael Jordan ended his 2001-2002 return season averaging 22.9 points, 5.7 rebounds, and 5.2 assists while shooting a respectably low 41.6% shooting clip. At 39 years old, he was still one of the greatest players in the world after making a trip to his 13th All-Star Game. And, even at his age, he was still a top-10 scorer in the league, ranking ninth behind Dirk Nowitzki in points per game average. Not bad for a 39-year old elder statesman.

The following year, Michael Jordan played all 82 games for the Washington Wizards, making him the only player on that roster to do so even though he had already reached the age of 40 during the middle of the season. Impressively, he broke the 40-point barrier three times during that season to make it known to the world that he was still a ridiculously good scorer.

Announcing that this would be his final season in the NBA, the fanfare that followed Michael Jordan all season long was amazing. He was voted in by coaches as a member of the 2003 Eastern Conference All-Stars but was not a starter. Nevertheless, Vince Carter eventually offered his starting spot to Jordan to give the greatest of all time the rightful farewell he deserved. MJ played his 14th All-Star Game and went on to pass Kareem Abdul-Jabbar as the midseason classic's greatest scorer at that time. (Both Kobe Bryant and LeBron James would later pass him in that regard.)

Michael Jordan played his final NBA game on April 16, 2003, at the age of 40. He played against the Philadelphia 76ers and scored only 15 points against Allen Iverson's team in a loss. The highlight of that game was when he went to the bench with four minutes left and was seemingly done. But the crowd chanted his name to the point that he had to come back with 2:35 left on the clock. He scored his final two points from the free-throw line and he was eventually given a three-minute standing ovation when he went back to the bench with more than a minute left on the clock.

The Washington Wizards never made it to the playoffs in those two years that Michael Jordan played for them. Nevertheless, having Jordan in that team gave them a chance. MJ averaged 20 points while shooting 44.5% from the floor in the 37 minutes a night that he played. Michael Jordan retired from the game of basketball still the NBA's all-time leader in points per game as he slightly edged out Wilt Chamberlain in that regard even after playing two more years with the Wizards.

Chapter 7: Post-Retirement Life

After Michael Jordan's final year as a player with the Washington Wizards, he thought that he would return to the front office as their president of basketball operations. However, he got fired by the Wizards' owner due to the series of unpopular decisions he made when he was the franchise's top executive. This included his drafting of Kwame Brown in 2001 and his trading of Rip Hamilton in 2002.

In 2006, Michael Jordan found himself in the NBA once again after buying a share of the Charlotte Bobcats, which later became known as the Hornets. While he may have only been the second-largest shareholder of the team, part of the purchase agreement was that he would take control over the franchise's basketball operations. Then in 2010, he finally became the majority owner of the Charlotte Bobcats franchise after striking a deal with the former majority owner.

As the owner of the Charlotte Bobcats/Hornets, Michael Jordan did not have a lot of success as far as team performance was concerned. However, he is credited for insightfully drafting point guard Kemba Walker, who was widely regarded as the greatest player the Charlotte Bobcats/Hornets ever had under the Michael Jordan ownership.

Chapter 8: Olympic Gold Standard

While the entire world knows that Michael Jordan was a member of the 1992 Dream Team that dominated the Olympic Games in Barcelona, not a lot of people know that his national team career started back in 1984 when he was fresh out of North Carolina and had just been drafted by the Chicago Bulls with the third overall pick. Back then, only amateur players were allowed to play in the Olympics. And since Jordan was yet to play his first NBA game, he was qualified to represent the United States in Los Angeles that year.

In the Los Angeles Olympic Games, Michael Jordan dominated the scoring end even though he was playing with fellow future NBA stars such as Patrick Ewing, Chris Mullin, and Alvin Robertson. Jordan averaged 17.1 points to lead the team in scoring. His best outing was when he scored 24 points against Spain during the Group B games. He scored 20 points in the gold medal game, which was once again versus Spain.

When the 1989 Olympic committee finally approved countries sending professional basketball players to represent them in the Olympic Games, this opened the floodgates for the U.S. to send what is widely considered the greatest basketball team ever assembled in the history of the sport. It was in 1991 when they decided to begin to put together the members of the team. The first 10 players selected included Michael Jordan and his fellow Bulls player, Scottie Pippen.

In 1992, the final two members of the team were selected. Clyde Drexler was selected over Isiah Thomas, which fueled speculation that Thomas had been left off that team due to his personal issues with Michael Jordan. However, it was much more probable that Drexler was selected over Thomas because he was still in the prime of his career while Isiah was already on the decline.[xlvi] However, that does not take away the fact that Isiah Thomas was just as deserving. It was just difficult to leave someone off to make way for the Pistons legend. Meanwhile, the final roster spot was reserved for the best collegiate player of that time. But, instead of going to Shaquille O'Neal, the selection committee decided to give the spot to Christian Laettner, who was the most successful player in college at that time.

When the final roster spots were set, the 1992 USA Olympic Men's Basketball Team was dubbed as "The Dream Team"—the greatest collection of talent the Olympics had ever seen. The final 12 were Michael Jordan, Magic Johnson, Larry Bird, Scottie Pippen, Charles Barkley, Karl Malone, John Stockton, Chris Mullin, Patrick Ewing, David Robinson, Clyde Drexler, and Christian Laettner.

It is widely posited that the greatest game Michael Jordan ever played in was not in the NBA, nor the Olympics, but in a practice game with the Dream Team. They were in Monte Carlo in preparation for the 1992 Olympic Games in Barcelona, Spain, and played a scrimmage with Jordan's White Team going up against Magic Johnson's Blue Team.

The White versus Blue practice game was described as the most intense game ever played by NBA players. Both Jordan and Magic were at their most competitive, even though Johnson had just retired from the game in 1991. The reason for the intensity was that Magic Johnson was not willing to cede his status as the captain of the Dream Team even though Michael Jordan was already by far the superior player of the two. Nevertheless, Jordan won out and scored 17 points.[xlvii] After what was considered the most intense game that featured Jordan, the members of the Dream Team hardly spoke to one another due to how they let it all out in that game. Nevertheless, they eventually started warming up to one another after earning each other's respect from the intensity of that hard-fought practice bout.

When the Dream Team finally arrived in Barcelona, they were treated like rock stars primarily because of how global an icon Michael Jordan already was at that point in his career. While the headliners of that squad included Magic and Larry, who both dominated the 1980s, it was still Jordan who the fans went out to see, particularly because of how his image and branding had transcended basketball and had permeated all facets of pop culture. Even people who had never watched a basketball game before in their lives were well aware of who Michael Jordan was.

It was during the Olympic Games that Michael Jordan and Scottie Pippen first saw what their future teammate Toni Kukoč was capable of. Prior to the Olympics, the Bulls had drafted Kukoč in the second round of the 1990 NBA Draft after impressing Jerry Krause, who infamously went on to say that Kukoč was going to be the future of the Chicago Bulls (a comment that understandably rubbed both Michael Jordan and Scottie Pippen the wrong way). Because Krause was giving more attention to Kukoč than the players he had in the team at that time, both Jordan and Pippen made it their mission to shut down the Croatian star during the Olympics. They even went on to say that nobody on that team other than them would guard Kukoč to make the point to Jerry Krause that they were a lot better than the Croatian star.[xlviii]

As expected, the Dream Team dominated the Olympics by beating all of their opponents with an average point differential of 43.7. While Michael Jordan was the team's number one option on offense and was taking most of the shots, it was Charles Barkley who went on to become their best player on offense during the entire tournament.

Nevertheless, Michael Jordan was the team's second-leading scorer and averaged 14.9 points, 2.4 rebounds, 4.8 assists, and 4.6 steals. Typical of Michael Jordan, his best performance of the tournament happened in the most important game in the gold medal round against Kukoč's Croatian team. He scored 22 points to help give the U.S. the gold medal in that tournament.

Overall, Michael Jordan is a two-time Olympic gold medalist but his best Olympic appearance was still in 1992 as the headliner of the legendary Dream Team. Michael Jordan helped make the game of basketball global by acting as an ambassador for the sport to the rest of the world.

Chapter 9: Michael Jordan's Impact and Legacy

When it comes right down to it, Michael Jordan's impact on the basketball world is something that words can never fully describe. That is how important a player he was in the history of the sport as he has gone from being a sensational athlete on the court to the game's greatest player of all time, not only in terms of his stats and accomplishments but also in terms of how he helped basketball evolve and become global.

As a shooting guard, Michael Jordan is arguably the most influential figure in terms of how the position evolved. Back in the years before Jordan, shooting guards were seen as catch-and-shoot players that would only dwell out in the perimeter and make jumpers whenever they could. That is why there have not been a lot of all-time great shooting guards prior to MJ's explosion in the NBA.

However, Michael Jordan came into the league as an entirely different breed of shooting guard. He was similar to George Gervin, a four-time scoring champion at the shooting guard spot, in the sense that he was able to get himself to the basket and finish with grace. However, he was also a lot closer to the legendary small forward Julius "Dr. J" Erving, whose scoring was predicated on his ability to use his athletic gifts to get close to the basket and finish strong.

The fact that Jordan had the grace of a Gervin and the athleticism of an Erving was something unheard of in the history of the sport in terms of what a shooting guard had to offer. And, throughout the early portion of his career, Michael Jordan stuck to that player profile and dominated opposing teams with his ability to get to the basket. He would add a few moves here and there but his game was always about using his athleticism to score points near the basket. That is why the early iterations of Michael Jordan were all about his athletic abilities and he was dubbed with names such as "Air Jordan" and "His Airness."

But, as Jordan began to realize the need for him to mix and match his offensive arsenal, he began dwelling more and more out on the perimeter to shoot jump shots. He always had a good jump shot, which he developed under Dean Smith in North Carolina, but he did not always go to his jumper unless there was a need for him to do so. There was even a time when the Chicago Bulls doubted his ability to hit jumpers with consistency.

Due to his hard work and intense competitive drive, Michael Jordan mastered the art of the jump shot and steadily incorporated the midrange game to his player profile until it turned into his most prolific weapon during his second stint with the Chicago Bulls. However, unlike the likes of classic and traditional shooting guards, he was not a catch-and-shoot player. Instead, his midrange game became a product of his ability to break defenders in one-on-one isolation plays either off the dribble from beyond the three-point line or from the post whenever he turned around for a fading jumper.

In that regard, with Jordan's ability to get to the basket and finish strong at the rim mixed with his astonishingly prolific midrange game the likes of which the NBA had never seen, he became a complete scorer who could beat opponents in virtually any situation. The only thing missing from his game was the three-pointer because, at that time during the 1990s, this was not a shot that coaches incorporated in their systems. However, had Jordan been born much later and played during the 2000s or even the 2010s, he would have surely incorporated the three-pointer into his bag of tricks to become an even more complete player at the shooting guard position.

All that considered, Michael Jordan's impact as a shooting guard cannot be overstated because he was the one single figure that helped inspire an entirely new breed of wing players. Kids during the 80s and 90s wanted to be "like Mike" and would emulate the way Jordan played. That was why the 1990s saw an influx of talented wings that all tried to play like Michael Jordan. He changed the way the game was being played and was the figure that inspired an entire generation of basketball players.

From being a league dominated by big men, the NBA moved to a more perimeter and isolation-oriented style of play during the 2000s when the new breed of Jordan-esque players came into the league. Guys like Vince Carter, Tracy McGrady, Paul Pierce, Dwyane Wade, and Allen Iverson all played the shooting guard and wing positions in a similar way to Jordan and they went on to become great scorers during an era that was steadily shying away from the post-up scoring all too prevalent during the 2000s.

However, out of all the "like Mike" players that followed after Jordan, Kobe Bryant remained the closest to MJ the world had ever seen. Bryant had always patterned his playing style to that of Jordan's. He got to the rim with his athletic gifts but, at the same time, mixed and matched his offensive arsenal with pull-up fadeaway jumpers and with post moves built on his otherworldly footwork.

Kobe became Mike's legacy player and MJ even went on to say that Bryant was the only player who could have beaten him one-on-one due to how he was able to pattern his game after the greatest player of all time.[xlix] The two legends became close friends, as Kobe Bryant spent a lot of his early days in the NBA asking Michael Jordan for tips. Jordan treated Bryant like a little brother and even went on to become one of the few people who gave a speech during Kobe's memorial service in Staples Center shortly after the Laker legend's death in January of 2020. Michael Jordan famously cried while giving a heart-wrenching, emotional speech in memory of his friend.

While Michael Jordan may have changed the way the game of basketball was being played, he was also the biggest figure that contributed to the massive growth in popularity of the NBA during the 80s and 90s. In the 80s, the rivalry between Magic Johnson and

Larry Bird was what contributed to the rise of the NBA after the league experienced what might be viewed as a dark age during the 1970s. However, following Johnson and Bird, it was Jordan who the NBA pounced on due to his massive success as an individual player who could inspire people all over the world with his athletic feats.

Jordan was a marketing icon who the NBA and Nike capitalized on for success. His Jordan brand allowed the athletic shoe industry to rise and evolve over the years as fans could not help but grab a pair of Michael's signature shoes in the hopes that they too would be able to play "like Mike." On top of that, Jordan's later success as a champion allowed fans from different countries to become witnesses to what true individual and team greatness was all about.

The culmination of his rise as a global icon came in the 1992 Olympic Games held in Spain as it was the first time that Michael Jordan truly understood how fans from all over the world embraced his greatness. Even when he was in Spain, his image and his popularity never wavered. It was as if he was still in America due to the warm reception he got from basketball fans coming from all over the world. It was then that the NBA knew they had the first true global basketball superstar in their hands.

That said, Michael Jordan's ability to inspire an entire generation of basketball players while contributing to the massive global growth of the NBA made him the most impactful superstar the league had ever seen. And, adding the fact that he was putting up fantastic stats while leading his Chicago Bulls team to championship after championship, it was easy to form a narrative that he had become the greatest basketball player ever to grace the court.

In the years that followed Jordan's retirement from the game of basketball, all of the NBA superstars that headlined the league year after year were always compared to MJ because he had set new standards for what an NBA superstar should be. Among those superstars, Kobe Bryant and LeBron James were the most prominent ones to ascend in the wake of his influence.

When Kobe Bryant retired from the game of basketball in 2016, he was a five-time NBA champion, an 18-time All-Star, and the league's third all-time leading scorer before LeBron passed him in 2020. He set the standard for what it was like to be like Jordan but he also made a name for himself, not as Mike's clone but as someone who carried the torch yet also had an identity and playing style that was uniquely his own.

Meanwhile, the one person who had truly been able to threaten Michael Jordan's place as the greatest of all time was LeBron James. When James entered into the league in 2003, he never had the pleasure of going up against Michael Jordan, unlike Kobe Bryant, but he was already crowned as the NBA's next big thing. This was largely due to James' ability to score dominantly from the wing position using his superior size and athletic ability while playing a style similar to that of Magic Johnson in terms of what he could do as a playmaker.

LeBron James lived up to the hype that surrounded him when he entered the league and became a four-time MVP and a multi-time champion while staying consistent as a performer from 2003.

However, while LeBron James may have subsequently carved up one of the greatest careers in the history of the NBA, there are still those who would measure his greatness to that of Michael Jordan's. LeBron may have ultimately scored more points, collected more rebounds, passed more assists, and appeared in more All-Star Games, but he has yet to measure up to the championships that Michael Jordan was able to win during the 1990s. And, while James may be a global icon in his own right, the impact that Michael Jordan has had, the fanfare that followed him wherever he went, and the mystique that surrounded him will always remain special and unparalleled. His popularity and influence continue to this day in a manner that is as far-reaching as it is timeless. And that is why he is still widely regarded as the GOAT of professional basketball.

It cannot be questioned that records were meant to be broken and that the success of past players will always be the stepping stone used by current and future superstars. That said, there can be no guarantee that Michael Jordan will remain the greatest, just as there was no guarantee that Bill Russell would remain the greatest, or Kareem Abdul-Jabbar. Basketball is a sport that perpetually evolves through the years as new players learn from their predecessors and try to achieve more than what their forebears were able to do. Every great superstar's legacy is a time capsule that reflects not only the player's unique gifts to the sport but also a special moment in the evolution of the NBA.

As such, it may be inevitable that someone will eventually take over the throne as the greatest of all time, but there can be no doubt in anyone's mind that Michael Jordan will always be the most iconic, electrifying player to have ever laced his equally iconic sneakers up. That is why, to this day, young people still want to "be like Mike.

Final Word/About the Author

Wow! You made it to the end of this book, and you're reading the About the Author section? Now that's impressive and puts you in the top 1% of readers.

Since you're curious about me, I was born and raised in Norwalk, Connecticut. Growing up, I could often be found spending many nights watching basketball, soccer, and football matches with my father in the family living room. I love sports and everything that sports can embody. I believe that sports are one of the most genuine forms of competition, heart, and determination. I write my works to learn more about influential athletes in the hopes that from my writing, you the reader can walk away inspired to put in an equal if not greater amount of hard work and perseverance to pursue your goals.

I've written these stories for over a decade, and loved every moment of it. When I look back on my life, I am most proud of not just having covered so many different athletes' inspirational stories, but for all the times I got e-mails or handwritten letters from readers on the impact my books have had on them.

So thank you from the bottom of my heart for allowing me to do work I find meaningful. I am incredibly grateful for you and your support.

If you're new to my sports biography books, welcome. I have goodies for you as a thank you from me in the pages ahead.

Before we get there though, I have a question for you...

Were you inspired at any point in this book?
If so, would you help someone else get inspired too?

You see, my mission is to inspire sports fans of all ages around the world that anything is possible through hard work and perseverance…but the only way to accomplish this mission is by reaching everyone.

So here's my ask from you:

Most people, regardless of what the saying tells them to do, judge a book by its cover (and its reviews).

If you enjoyed *Michael Jordan: The Inspiring Story of One of Basketball's Greatest Players,* please help inspire another person needing to hear this story by leaving a review.

Doing so takes less than a minute, and that dose of inspiration can change another person's life in more ways than you can even imagine.

To get that generous 'feel good' feeling and help another person, all you have to do is take 60 seconds and leave a review.

If you're on Audible: hit the three dots in the top right of your device, click rate & review, then leave a few sentences about the book with a star rating.

If you're reading on Kindle or an e-reader: scroll to the bottom of the book, then swipe up and it will prompt a review for you.

If for some reason these have changed: you can head back to Amazon and leave a review right on the book's page.

Thank you for helping another person, and for your support of my writing as an independent author.

Clayton

Like what you read?
Then you'll love these too!

This book is one of hundreds of stories I've written. If you enjoyed this story on Michael Jordan, you'll love my other sports biography book series too.

You can find them by visiting my website at claytongeoffreys.com or by scanning the QR code below to follow my author page on Amazon.

Here's a little teaser about each of my sports biography book series:

Basketball Biography Books: This series covers the stories of over 100 NBA greats such as Stephen Curry, LeBron James, Michael Jordan, and more.

Basketball Leadership Biography Books: This series covers the stories of basketball coaching greats such as Steve Kerr, Gregg Popovich, John Wooden, and more.

Football Biography Books: This series covers the stories of over 50 NFL greats such as Peyton Manning, Tom Brady, and Patrick Mahomes, and more.

Baseball Biography Books: This series covers the stories of over 40 MLB greats such as Aaron Judge, Shohei Ohtani, Mike Trout, and more.

Soccer Biography Books: This series covers the stories of tennis greats such as Neymar, Harry Kane, Robert Lewandowski, and more.

Tennis Biography Books: This series covers the stories of tennis greats such as Serena Williams, Rafael Nadal, Andy Roddick, and more.

Women's Basketball Biography Books: This series covers the stories of many WNBA greats such as Diana Taurasi, Sue Bird, Sabrina Ionescu, and more.

Lastly, if you'd like to join my exclusive list where I let you know about my latest books, and gift you free copies of some of my other books, go to **claytongeoffreys.com/goodies**.

Or, if you don't like typing, scan the following QR code here to go there directly. See you there!

Clayton

References

[i] Reeves, Ed. "Michael Jordan's Brother Helped to Instill His Legendary Competitiveness". *Sports Casting*. 5 March 2020. Web.

[ii] Milord, Joseph. "Had He Been Taller, Michael Jordan's Brother Would Have Been The Greatest Ever". *Elite Daily*. 1 August 2014. Web.

[iii] Isaacson, Melissa. "Portrait of a legend". *ESPN*. 9 September 2009. Web.

[iv] "Michael Jordan Didn't Make Varsity—At First". *Newsweek*. 17 October 2015. Web.

[v] Torres, Aaron. "Roy Williams shares incredible story of how UNC landed Michael Jordan". *Fox Sports*. 20 January 2017. Web.

[vi] Krest, Shawn. "Three Things: A Letter From Coach Smith". *WRAL.com*. 5 June 2017. Web.

[vii] Weinbach, Jake. "The Last Dance: Michael Jordan wouldn't be Jordan without Dean Smith". *Hoops Habit*. 21 March 2020. Web.

[viii] Zillgitt, Jeff. "What if Michael Jordan was drafted by the Portland Trail Blazers in 1984?". *USA Today*. 19 May 2020. Web.

[ix] Rovell, Darren. "How Nike landed Michael Jordan". *ESPN*. 15 February 2013. Web.

[x] Schaefer, Rob. "How Michael Jordan's agent played a role in 1985 NBA All-Star freezeout". *NBC Sports*. 11 February 2020. Web.

[xi] Lauletta, Tyler. "31 things we learned about Michael Jordan and the 1998 Chicago Bulls in "The Last Dance"". *Insider*. 19 May 2020. Web.

[xii] Walker, Rhiannon. "The day Larry Bird said, 'It's just God disguised as Michael Jordan'". *The Undefeated*. 18 April 2018. Web.

[xiii] Canova, Daniel. "Scottie Pippen convinced Bulls GM Jerry Krause to trade up for him in 1987 NBA Draft". *Fox News*. 11 May 2020. Web.

[xiv] Herbert, James. "The Jordan Rules: What 'The Last Dance' documentary doesn't say about Pistons' defense against Michael Jordan". *CBS Sports*. 15 May 2020. Web.

[xv] Herbert, James. "Michael Jordan hits 'The Shot' over Craig Ehlo: What 'The Last Dance' doesn't say about iconic Bulls moment". *CBS Sports*. 17 May 2020. Web.

[xvi] Black, Ryan. "Kansas State legend Tex Winter remembered as 'finest offensive mind in basketball' during 'The Last Dance'". *The Mercury*. 27 April 2020. Web.

[xvii] Anderson, Austin. "'The Last Dance': 3 things we learned from second night of Michael Jordan documentary". *Sporting News*. 27 April 2020. Web.

[xviii] Medina, Mark. "Day 47 without sports: How Phil Jackson convinced Michael Jordan to buy into his philosophy". *USA Today*. 27 April 2020.

Web.

xix Davis, Scott. "Michael Jordan once added 15 pounds of muscle in one summer to prepare for a rival and changed the way athletes train". *Insider*. 28 April 2020. Web.

xx Blackburn, Pete. "How Isiah Thomas' explanation for the Pistons walk-off has evolved over the years". *CBS Sports*. 27 April 2020. Web.

xxi Mickanen, Dylan. "Social media reacts to Michael Jordan's disrespect of Clyde Drexler in 'The Last Dance'". *NBC Sports*. 3 May 2020. Web.

xxii Dodson, Aaron. "On this day in NBA Finals history: Michael Jordan's 'Shrug Game'". *The Undefeated*. 3 June 2017. Web.

xxiii Helin, Kurt. "Last Dance gets into Bulls-Knicks rivalry: 'It wasn't really a foul until you drew blood'". *NBC Sports*. 4 May 2020. Web.

xxiv McIntyre, Jason. "How Michael Jordan's Atlantic City gambling trip paved the way for his first retirement". *Fox Sports*. 4 May 2020. Web.

xxv Smith, Sam. "Barkley: NBA championship is our destiny". *Chicago Tribune*. 19 June 1993. Web.

xxvi Martin. "'I believe we killed Michael Jordan's dad'". *Chicago Tribune*. 4 January 1996. Web.

xxvii McCallum, Jack. "'The desire isn't there'". *Sports Illustrated*. 18 October 1993. Web.

xxviii Poole, Monte. "Michael Jordan's baseball detour was one final gift to his late dad". *NBC Sports*. 11 May 2020. Web.

xxix Fagan, Ryan. "Was Michael Jordan good at baseball? A look back on his brief career with the White Sox". *Sporting News*. 11 May 2020. Web.

xxx Reynolds, Tim. "A breakfast in 1995 played a role in Jordan's NBA return". *NBA.com*. 11 May 2020. Web.

xxxi De Silva, Bodie. "Former Poway star Jud Buechler talks about 'The Last Dance' and playing with Michael Jordan: 'The crowds, the people, it was crazy'". *Scorebook live*. 17 May 2020. Web.

xxxii Smith, Sam. ""I'm back" – Michael Jordan's famous return to basketball". *NBA.com*. 19 March 2020. Web.

xxxiii Walks, Matt. "Flashback: 20 years ago today, Anderson forces MJ back to No. 23". *NBA.com*. 8 May 2015. Web.

xxxiv Elkins, Kathleen. "Michael Jordan trained 5 hours a day while also filming 'Space Jam' from 7 a.m. to 7 p.m.". *NBC*. 18 May 2020. Web.

xxxv Scaletta, Kelly. "How Michael Jordan re-defined his game to extend his legendary career". *Bleacher Report*. 22 August 2013. Web.

xxxvi Goldsberry, Kirk. "Why Michael Jordan's scoring prowess still can't be touched". *ESPN*. 20 May 2020. Web.

xxxvii Fernandez, Gabriel. "How the legend of Michael Jordan's 'flu game' has evolved since the 1997 NBA Finals". *CBS Sports*. 20 May 2020. Web.

xxxviii Sherman, Rodger. "How Much Credit and Blame Does Jerry Krause Really Deserve?". *The Ringer*. 12 May 2020. Web.

xxxix Herbert, James. "Michael Jordan-Kobe Bryant connection: What 'The Last Dance' doc doesn't mention about their relationship". *CBS Sports*. 15 May 2020. Web.

xl Chavez, Chris. "Michael Jordan Didn't Fly To Vegas To Pick Up Dennis Rodman". *Sports Illustrated*. 27 April 2020. Web.

xli Baer, Jack. "Reggie Miller admits he 'lightly' pushed off Michael Jordan in 1998 Eastern Conference finals". *Yahoo Sports*. 18 May 2020. Web.

xlii Banks, Lacy. "Pippen's pain, sweat, and tears". *Chicago Sun-Times*. 15 June 1998. Web.

xliii Botkin, Brad. "Michael Jordan didn't retire just because of Jerry Krause, who continues to be disproportionately vilified". *CBS Sports*. 6 May 2020. Web.

xliv "Jordan watched Lemieux's comeback very closely". *ESPN*. 2 October 2001. Web.

xlv "Top Moments: Michael Jordan returns to NBA at age 38". *NBA.com*. Web.

xlvi Whitaker, Lang. "The Dream Will Never Die: An Oral History of the Dream Team". *GQ*. 11 June 2012. Web.

xlvii Estevez, Juan. "The greatest game Michael Jordan ever played in: The Dream Team practice in Monte Carlo". *NBA.com*. 2 May 2020. Web.

xlviii Santaromita, Dan. "Michael Jordan and Scottie Pippen's dominant Olympics statement vs. Toni Kukoc". *NBC Sports*. 22 April 2020. Web.

xlix Rohlin, Melissa. "Michael Jordan Says Kobe Bryant Could've Beaten Him One-On-One". *Sports Illustrated*. 25 April 2020. Web.

Made in United States
Orlando, FL
21 April 2024

46040562R00095